I0201444

Heaven Heals a Codependent's Heart

Diane Vernitsky Jellen

Copyright © 2017 by Diane M. Jellen

All rights reserved. No part of this publication may be reproduced in any form without written permission from the author or publisher.

Unless otherwise indicated, all Scripture quotations are taken from the Holy Bible, New Living Translation, copyright © 1996, 2004, 2007 by Tyndale House Foundation. Used by permission of Tyndale House Publishers, Inc., Carol Stream, Illinois 60188. All rights reserved.

Scripture marked CEV is taken from the Contemporary English Version® Copyright © 1995 American Bible Society. All rights reserved.

Scripture marked MSG is taken from *The Message*. Copyright © 1993, 1994, 1995, 1996, 2000, 2001, 2002. Used by permission of NavPress Publishing Group.

Scripture marked NASB is taken from the New American Standard Bible®. Copyright© 1960, 1962, 1963, 1968, 1971, 1972, 1973, 1975, 1977, 1995, by The Lockman Foundation. Used by permission.

Scripture marked NKJV is taken from the New King James Version®. Copyright © 1982 by Thomas Nelson, Inc. Used by permission. All rights reserved.

All events in this memoir are fact; however, several have been condensed, and several names and locations have been changed to ensure anonymity and to respect the confidentiality of others.

Dedication

To my Mother and *Dziadzi* (Polish for grandfather). Thank you for guiding me on the steps to decency. Your firm footprints led me to a loving Father God—a divine Higher Power greater than myself. In Him, I found the steps to wholeness.

To the recovering co-addicts and addicts who continue to join me on the steps to a healthier way of life.

Contents

Introduction

The Journey

"Let's see how close you can come to erasing my steps," I taunt the rough ocean beside me.

Suntanned toes burrow in the soft white sand. A narrow instep and a heavy heel complete the footprint. The footprints trudge forward, desperately trying to walk a straight line.

Those footprints are mine. My footprints are different from the twig-like zigzag pattern left by seagulls scavenging for breakfast. Both sets of footprints dance dangerously close to the incoming tide, tempting the waves to try to catch them.

It is all about the timing. A quick jump at the right time will keep the frothy seawater from reaching my footprints—and me. I pride myself on being quick, a survivor who can handle anything and walk away nursing my wounds. All by myself. At times, however, the always-in-control lies I tell myself catch me off guard.

Oh no, I waited too long. I misjudged the speed of the ice blue waves! The chilly sea takes out my footprints and recedes into the endless Atlantic.

Yet, I am not discouraged. I have had much practice tempting fate. You see, I have done this same thing before. I did this yesterday. And the day before that. And the day before *that*. Like most codependents, I have been conditioned to test my denial skills one day at a time. Each day the situation changes. Each day brings a new step— a new story. Each will leave a unique imprint.

The Healing

My first book, *My Resurrected Heart: A Codependent's Journey to Healing,* tells the story of a young couple very much in love with each other and the party scene. This love story had every hope of ending happily ever after. It did not. In the book, I held nothing back as I recalled how my husband and I unsuspectingly allowed denial to rule our lives. I introduced to readers Ms. Miller Lite, the "other woman" in our marriage. Over the years, this couple maneuvered around many roadblocks. Snarled in the unexpected twists and turns, one partner turned to a 12 Step Program. The other partner claimed he did not have a problem. "I'm fine, Diane. Why do you always have to create a problem where there isn't one?"

The forty-day journal stories in *My Resurrected Heart* made clear to readers that all was not fine.

The impressions I share here in the sequel to *My Resurrected Heart* follow the footprints of those I encountered along the timeless, shifting sands of recovery. Beginning with the dreary November afternoon when my husband packed his bags, grabbed denial by the hand, and walked out the door. Just like that, one set of husband and wife footprints washed away—forever.

One set of footsteps, however, regained its footing and limped on.

You walked through the water of the mighty sea, but your footprints were never seen (Psalm 77:19 CEV).

Part One: The Perfect Storm

1. Lifeline to Living

The Journey

"No, I don't know where he is going to live or when I'll see him again," I cried.

Hairspray dampened by perspiration glued the phone to the side of my head, making a sticky situation worse. I was talking to my daughter Kellyann. I would have done anything not to be the one to tell her that her daddy and I had separated. My daughter had only been married for two months. A newlywed who should have been excited about her new role as a wife, now she found herself caught up in the drama of her parents' failed marriage. Although Kellyann lived in Florida, her footprints still intertwined in our family saga. It was my job to call and tell her Daddy and I had fallen out of step.

The dissolution of almost three decades of marriage caught Kellyann by surprise. Stunned, she asked to know more. I needed to know more too. I felt I deserved an explanation myself.

None was coming.

After I hung up, the deafening silence of the drab stone walls of our century-old farmhouse screamed in my ears. I had to get out of there. My teenage son was in his room, so I shouted up the circular pine staircase. "Jonathan, I cannot be in this house another minute without Dad. Let's go for a drive."

"Mom, you go. I want to stay here."

He did not say "alone," but I later learned there are many roles the children of addicts adopt. Jonathan mirrored the Lost Child Role. His denial directed him to languish in the background and appear indifferent to the pain around him.

Jonathan contends his actions were due to acceptance rather than denial.

The Healing

Autumn was always my least favorite season of the year because it signaled the end of daylight saving time. It was 5 PM and the sun had already set.

Evening darkened the countryside as I drove the winding roads looking for peace. Searching for hope. Was it possible I could find a bright new beginning around the next bend? I need a fresh start. Anything that could give me a reason to go on. Each turn painted a scene of summer's death. Bountiful fields once full of proud stalks of sweet corn had produced dried stumps of straw.

Depressing thoughts threatened to overtake me. I shifted gears and tried to focus on my children. I thought about Paul and Jonathan, and I scolded myself. *You're not the only one hurting. The kids are just as confused. You shouldn't have left Jonathan alone. And did you stop to think how Paul will react when he comes home and finds both of his parents gone?*

The next intersection provided me with clear direction markers. No matter where or how fast I drive, I cannot outrun the truth.

Thanks to power steering, I maneuvered a U-turn on the narrow road. Every bend that led me back home brought gales of confusion as I questioned the course my marriage had traveled. Staying true to my wedding vows was the lifeline that was supposed to protect us when our stormy marriage blew out of control. I questioned God. *If You were in this with me, Lord, why didn't you save us from this disaster?* Mark 4:35-38 tells the story of when Jesus and His disciples were crossing the Sea of Galilee with several smaller boats. Jesus was asleep when a violent windstorm arose. Their faith shaken, the disciples panicked and woke Him.

Even though the night was clear, I too was in the midst of a storm. Along with trying to keep my marriage together, my need to help others often placed me in the middle of a squall. I have since learned I cannot save the "smaller boats" of family and friends in crisis. We all have access to the same God who is willing to guide us through the tempests of life. It is up to each of us to turn our lives around and allow Him to calm our fears. His disciples did not perish, and neither will we.

"...Teacher, don't you care that we're going to drown?"
(Mark 4:38).

Notes:

2. A Cushion Calms the Fear

The Journey

Sleep. The only escape from my living nightmare. On my way home, I counted on sleep to be my safe harbor. Exhausted from the drama of Bob moving out, I promised myself if the boys were okay when I got home, I would make them a quick meal and go right to bed.

When I arrived home, Jonathan assured me he was doing fine. In a subdued voice, he added, "Paul called. He's eating at his girlfriend's house."

I had lost all sense of time. On a normal Saturday in November, the aroma of a hearty beef stew would have filled our home. Today, cooking was the last thing I wanted to do. But Jonathan had not eaten. It was time to concentrate on his needs.

"Jonathan, I don't have the energy to cook. Let's go out to supper."

"No, I'm okay. I'm not hungry."

"Still, I think we should eat. Grab your coat. Let's go get a pizza." His favorite meal.

In a comfy booth at a local Italian restaurant, Jonathan managed to relax enough to eat several slices of pizza. I pushed the food around on my plate. Jabbing a forkful of salad, then knocking it off, repeating the same motion with a piece of Italian sausage. There was nothing on my plate that would satisfy my craving for stability.

I could not force myself to eat. My mind was busy trying to accept the next step. I knew what I had to do. It was time to call an attorney.

The Healing

This realistic plan of action cut deeply as if I'd picked up a dinner knife and cut my "'till death do us part" vow into tiny pieces. After years of trying to keep my marriage afloat, talking to a lawyer would mean admitting I'd failed. My hard work had meant nothing. I sat and stared at a meal I could never digest.

An inner voice of faith interrupted my whirling thoughts. *Diane, it saddens God to see you working so hard and trusting Him so little.*

I didn't listen. From an early age, I'd always thought I had to be in control. I knew there was a God, but believed it would be my works that would prove my worth. I didn't know I had a Higher Power working on my behalf.

Trust. Was that the lesson Jesus wanted me to learn? Jesus trusted His Father. Trust was what He tried to teach His followers as He slept through the storm "with His head on a cushion" (Mark 4:38).

I often told my therapist, "I just want to sleep, and wake up when all my problems are solved." Now I understand how this type of sleep is not rest but avoidance. This form of sleep is depression. The kind of sleep that offers no refreshment to the soul.

After a weak attempt to nourish our bodies, my son and I went home. Jonathan provided a strong silent hug, which is his trademark, then he went upstairs. With the colorful afghan Aunt Violet had crocheted for me wrapped around my shoulders, I snuggled into the loveseat and stared into the comfortless night.

There was nothing to see, but something felt different. Soft cracking sounds relieved the tension in my neck as I moved my head from side to side. With each twist, menacing thoughts began to dissipate. Sitting in a living room filled with shadows, I felt a sense of peace. Finally, I admitted there was nothing more I could do to change my husband's decision. The only control I had was over my own actions going forward.

The emotional storm had passed. I had survived.

Tonight, I wouldn't have to search the black horizon for

headlights from Bob's car to guide him safely home from the bar. Tonight, I might be able to go to sleep without worrying. Tonight, I just may get a good night's rest.

Years have passed since that difficult night, but whenever I read the Scripture story of Jesus sleeping in the back of a boat in the middle of a powerful storm, I think of my own stormy night. And I still wonder, where did He get the cushion? Really, Jesus, where did you get that pillow?

One thing I do know is this: I no longer have to ride out the storms of my life alone. I have learned to grab my cushion of comfort and rest in Him. He is the Perfect Storm who will bring us safely home.

> *But soon a fierce storm came up. High waves were breaking into the boat, and it began to fill with water. Jesus was sleeping at the back of the boat with his head on a cushion...* (Mark 4:37-38)

Notes:

Part Two: Fire Drill or Faith Drill

3. A Call to Listen

The Journey

"Here, I made this just for you. Eat it. You'll feel better."

Food, food, and more delicious home-cooked food. This was my mother's remedy for pleasing others, which in turn endorsed her purpose in life. Mom had the ideal job that allowed her to share her prescription for healthy living. A self-taught stick-to-your-ribs kind of cook, she worked at a Roman Catholic rectory and treated the six priests she served as if they were her own sons. There was prayer before each meal, but with Mom's mouth-watering entrees in front of them, I doubt the priests entertained fasting.

It was only natural for caregiver Mom to worry about the unfolding drama in my family. One night she called to say she had arranged to have her favorite priest, Father Jim, meet with me in his office to provide counsel regarding my marital breakup. I knew he was doing her a favor, and on the night we met I came right to the point.

"Father Jim, I know God is asking me to let go of Bob, just as He asked Abraham to offer up his son, Isaac." Between sobs, I managed to add, "I'm confident when God is finished testing my faith, He will give me back a sober husband."

My distorted idea to surrender my spouse came from the first book of the Bible. In Genesis, chapter 22, God tested Abraham's faith by calling him to take his only son Isaac and sacrifice him as a burnt offering. Abraham agreed, and the following morning Isaac carried the wood as they set out for Mt. Moriah. When they arrived, Isaac questioned his dad. *"We have the fire and the wood,"* the boy said, *"but where is the sheep for the burnt offering?" "God will provide a sheep for the burnt offering, my son,"* Abraham answered. (Genesis 22:7-8)

The melodrama builds from there. At the last second, as Abraham raised up his knife to sacrifice his son, God stopped him.

11

Abraham had passed the test. God spared Isaac.

I believed Bob would stop drinking in this same way so that, at the very last second the miracle would happen. We would not have to sacrifice our marriage. We could live happily ever after.

Dressed in the traditional black slacks and clerical collared shirt, the priest patiently listened to my version of the Scripture story. He folded and unfolded his hands, adjusted his reading glasses several times, but he never interrupted me. I was grateful because it was important that he hear my side of the story. I talked so much, however, I didn't allow him any time to counsel me. The one comment Father Jim did make was this: "How interesting that you would compare yourself and your husband with this particular Bible story."

Great, he agrees with me, I thought.

Confident the priest was impressed with my deep faith, I left his office convinced everything would work out according to my interpretation. All would be fine, just as it had been for Abraham.

My marriage would be spared.

The Healing

Like most high-strung enablers, I tried to conceal my fears with nervous chatter. Unaware of the power denial played in my behavior, I continued to ignore the underlying truth. My self-protective nature demanded I have all the answers for any situation that arose in my life.

I carried this practice into my prayer time. I told God what I needed and asked for His help. If His answers were slow in coming, I figured out my own strategy and moved on before He could respond. But my Father God was listening. He always listens. Yet, when He was ready to speak to my spirit, I was gone. I could picture God scratching His head, looking around and asking, "Now where did she go? I wanted to talk to her."

Al-Anon's 12 Step recovery program taught me the art of serenity, how to be still and listen. When I took the time to settle my soul, I heard my Abba Father's gentle voice calling *me* to walk with Him, just as Isaac walked with his dad. In awe, I accepted His call.

Clumsy at first, my footing improved and, with ever-steadier footprints, I began to move forward.

Some time later, God tested Abraham's faith. "Abraham!" God called. "Yes," he replied. "Here I am." "Take your son, your only son—yes, Isaac, whom you love so much—and go to the land of Moriah. Go and sacrifice him as a burnt offering on one of the mountains, which I will show you" (Genesis 22:1-2).

Notes:

4. Faith in Action

The Journey

Vivid Scripture set the scene for Abraham's unthinkable task, but I read between the lines and uncovered a victim mentality story. It was only natural I would identify with this man. I ignored the fact that Abraham was dealing with his son. Only later did I realize that, due to my self-sacrificing nature, I was treating my dependent spouse as though he were my child. It was time for someone in this family to grow up.

I decided *I* would be that someone.

Just as Abraham followed the plan God had for his life, I believed God had a design for my family too. The unpredictability of living with an addict makes it impossible to focus on any sensible plan. My enabling, however, was predictable. All I had to do was to continue to fit each situation into the outcome I wanted for my family. That meant twisting each crisis to reach a not-so-calm diplomatic solution. If I didn't act to keep everything in place, all I valued and loved would be lost. I was sure of it.

Isaac believed in the cultural tradition of sacrificing animals, and he followed his father up the mountain. Somehow, this particular journey felt different. Human sacrifice was not part of their accepted belief. Isaac's uneasiness was too great to ignore. He trusted his instincts, but it was his innocence that prompted the boy to ask, "Where is the lamb?" (Genesis 22:7 NKJV).

Unlike Isaac, I did not have the courage to question a lifetime of uncomfortable situations. Years of sheltering the dependents in my life weakened my ability to protect myself. I knew my marriage could explode at any moment, but I didn't know my need to control was the accelerant that fueled the tinder box. I refused to quit. Obsessive caregivers don't quit. A dependable codependent never gives up.

Looking back after years of self-discovery, I can see how Father

Jim's perception of my identification with the sacrificial victim was right on the mark.

The Healing

If I could have questioned these two biblical figures, I would have asked Abraham, "Were you in denial? Did you pretend everything would turn out okay? Was your faith so grounded, you knew God would honor your obedience and spare your son at the last minute?" And you, Isaac. "If you were strong enough to carry the wood for the sacrifice, would you lie down willingly or would you put up a fight?"

Not surprising, I saved the most difficult questions for myself. Why did I continue to doubt God when I knew deep inside He had laid down His life for me?

Isaac asked, "where is the lamb," and I did the same. With the help of support groups, I summoned the courage to ask, "What is really going on here?" I needed to know why, when my spouse's drinking increased, my trust in my Higher Power decreased.

Each question I asked led to new insights. Calmness stepped in and taught me to trust my instincts. God's plan had a truth embedded in it that I had chosen to ignore. Like Abraham, I wanted to pass the test of obedience. However, before I could unload my burden, I would have to accept the truth. The truth was this: God based His plan for my life on *His* principles, not mine.

> *Isaac turned to Abraham and said, "Father?" "Yes, my son?" Abraham replied. "We have the fire and the wood," the boy said, "but where is the sheep for the burnt offering?" "God will provide a sheep for the burnt offering, my son," Abraham answered. And they both walked on together* (Genesis 22:7-8).

Part Three: Filling the Empty Nest Syndrome

5. Two Families Nesting

The Journey

The study of addiction equipped me with new insights. One detail I gleaned is this: the dis-ease of codependency—my need to fix others—lured me to the foot of many mountains that were not mine to scale. On my recovery path, I bumped into women with similar stories. Women who had just separated or were in the process of filing for divorce. Some had young children, others were alone with nowhere to live. Without sacrificing my own needs, I made the decision to help whenever possible.

Jonathan and I were not the typical empty nesters. In our house, it was a mother and her youngest son. The two of us were what was left of a once happy, animated family of six.

When our family split, cheerfulness also made an exit. Gone was the fun and laughter when my husband and our four kids shared summer evenings on the screened-in porch. Happy times when storytelling competed with the crickets' melodious song. All this ended when Bob moved into his mid-life crisis apartment. Kellyann and Rob soon followed, heading out on separate paths to their own futures. Then Paul went off to college.

Jonathan and I remained behind, struggling to create a new direction for our lives. Our voices echoed off the cold fieldstone walls. Many days I was haunted by one thought: *Next year he'll be off to college, and I will be all alone.*

Until that day came, I tried to support Jonathan in every way I could. Together, we looked for a used car to get him to school and work. On Saturdays, I cheered as he competed in high school track events. And after church on Sundays, Jonathan's girlfriend joined us for dinner.

One day after school, Jonathan shared his concern about a friend. "Mom, Kyle told me today his parents have separated."

"Oh, no," I cried. It always broke my heart when I heard about another family torn apart. My first thought was for the kids, caught in the middle of the painful crisis. "How are Kyle and his sister handling their parents' breakup?"

"Kyle seems okay. He said until the divorce is final and the judge decides which parent will keep the family home, Mrs. Regal is living in a rented room in town. The kids are staying in the house with their dad."

What?

"Jonathan, that is not okay. It's just not fair." It's not as if we had been close friends. I had only met Mrs. Regal at school functions, so I didn't know her well. Nonetheless, my take-charge attitude kicked in. "Call Kyle right now. Tell him that his mom can move into the empty bedroom at our house."

Within days, Bernice Regal had become our houseguest.

Friday after work, Bernice picked up her nine-year-old for a weekend sleepover. I cannot imagine the agony she must have felt on Sunday evening when Kimmy cried, "Mommy, please don't make me go home. We could share your bedroom. Please, please let me stay with you."

There would be no objections from me. This was a no-brainer. Kimmy and her mom were both welcome to stay.

Later that week, Bernice asked if Kyle could move in too. Why not? He could sleep on the pullout sofa in the den.

Without a fuss, Kyle had his own room down the hall from his sister and mother.

The Healing

Propelled from their own home by circumstances beyond their control, Bernice and her children settled into their new living quarters. Within confined borders, the five of us ricocheted through the house like pinballs trying to find a safe niche. Sleepy but with spirits high, we zipped through a tight morning schedule. Mindful of conserving hot water, we took quick showers. Then we nuked an instant oatmeal or grabbed a breakfast bar, before making a lively exodus to school or work.

As Bernice and I got to know each other, I admired her intelligence. She had a high-level position with an accounting firm. Bernice was also a free-spirited world traveler with varied cultural interests. How had she found herself in this intolerable situation?

In my case, it seemed obvious. I'd married young, raised four kids, and my husband drank a little too much. My job had me answering calls at the switchboard at a pharmaceutical company. And at forty-eight years old, I had just entered my second semester at the community college.

I rethought the judgements I had made about myself. Bernice's situation made it clear to me that dysfunction and divorce did not discriminate by class or education.

One night after school I dragged home, tired and hungry. When I opened the front door, the aroma of a fine Italian restaurant bubbled over to greet me. I inhaled the delicious smell of garlic, basil, and fresh tomato sauce.

Please God, don't let this be a dream.

In the dining room, Bernice, Kyle, Kimmy, and Jonathan were busy putting fresh-baked rolls in a basket. A ceramic pan of bubbling lasagna was the table's crowning centerpiece. The accomplished smiles on the kids' faces brought tears to my eyes. Lightheartedness filled the room, and overflowed into my heart. The contentment and gratitude I saw in the eyes of this makeshift family would stay with me forever.

The house was alive with a new, albeit untraditional, set of siblings and housemothers. The kids seemed relaxed in their new blended family. Life had thrust all of us onto a path, not of our choosing, but our resilient personalities had managed to spring back. With the grace of God, we maintained our emotional stability.

After the judge ruled in Bernice's favor, she and her two kids moved back into their home. Once again, I saw how the rooms of God's heart opened wide and dispelled my doubts. In the middle of my crisis, *Jehovah-Jireh*, our provider sustained my family and protected Bernice and her children.

> *"The servant returned and told his master what they had said. His master was furious and said, 'Go quickly into the streets and alleys of the town and invite the poor, the crippled, the blind, and the lame.' After the servant had done this, he reported, 'There is still room for more.' So his master said, 'Go out into the country lanes and behind the hedges and urge anyone you find to come, so that the house will be full'" (Luke 14:21-23).*

6. A Nest Egg Full of Pennies

The Journey

The newspaper ad read: For Rent, Apartment, Private Entrance.
Nobody had responded to the classified ad I ran in the newspaper. I turned to my neighbor for advice, telling Alice, "Now that Jonathan's gone off to college, I have two rooms I can rent out. I am counting on the extra income to help pay the bills."

With her usual confidence, my neighbor calmed me with a quote from Psalm 50. "Diane, He cares for the 'cattle on a thousand hills.' What makes you think He won't provide for you?"

Alice was right. God had taken care of me all these years. I prayed I would be okay. Still, I had to face my doubts—alone, in a house full of buried dreams.

Then a friend told me about Ellen, a local woman going through a divorce. Until they legally divided their property, Ellen did not want to live in the same house with her husband anymore. She needed a temporary place to stay.

The day after Christmas, Ellen moved in with me.

Every Friday after work, we had dinner together. We would joke about our culinary skills as we consumed a freezer-to-oven pizza or store-bought hoagies dripping with oil and vinegar. Between bites, we talked about our workweek, our kids, and what movie we would go see on Saturday. Our mealtime conversations always ended with two middle-aged women, exhausted but giggling about the silliest things. Laughing allowed us a release before we turned to the unsavory portion set before us. We'd discuss the status of our pending divorces and the dreaded asset distributions.

One evening Ellen confessed, "Jeff told his lawyer I took his penny jar when I moved out. He wants me to return it."

I tried not to laugh. "Did you take the penny jar?"

"Yes, but I'm not giving it back." She was serious.

"Ellen, you have a family homestead and other major assets to resolve. Why would you want to fight over a jar of pennies?"

"Why?" She scowled. "I'll tell you why. Because there are more than just pennies in Jeff's precious five-gallon jug. It's full of nickels, dimes, and quarters. I'm keeping it as a bargaining tool in our negotiations."

My guilty conscience grumbled. "Well, since we're guarding our nickels and dimes, please don't tell anyone you're paying me rent. If Bob finds out, he'll claim it's income and drag me back to court to renegotiate the amount he has to pay for the boys' college tuition."

The Healing

My new circle of friends consisted of desperate females, all of us attempting to maintain the thread of sanity by making insane excuses. I was quick to pass judgment on Ellen for holding Jeff's penny jar as ransom. Meanwhile, I tried to hide the paltry $50 in rent I collected from her each week. I needed the money. I didn't need the lies. Because of our predicament, however, deception seemed to be the only way any of us could protect what we believed belonged to us. If I had trusted in God's provision, I wouldn't have had to lie over penny ante stakes. God knew my needs and He would provide. His rewards were not monetary. He would restore the one gift worth reclaiming—my God-given integrity.

> *Aren't two sparrows sold for only a penny? But your Father knows when any one of them falls to the ground. Even the hairs on your head are counted. So don't be afraid! You are worth much more than many sparrows* (Matthew 10:29-31 CEV).

7. Swapping One Nest for Another

The Journey

An epidemic. That's what it was, a fast-spreading epidemic. Plague-ridden marriages ravaging the neighborhood. Displaced wives in search of shelter. Children torn between homes.

By opening my home as a safe haven for women in transition, I was practicing a principle of hope. Without realizing it, I was working the 12th Step, *Having had a spiritual awakening as the result of these steps, we tried to carry this message to others, and to practice these principles in all our affairs.*

After her divorce and financial settlement, Ellen bought a new condo in town. I would miss her. Before I had time to worry about the loss of weekly rent, however, Sarah moved in.

After her twenty-five-year marriage ended, Sarah had been desperate. Ignoring the recommended quarantine period of adjustment for divorcees, she met a guy and hastily said, "I do." Almost as quickly, her second marriage displayed symptoms of the plague. Second divorce pending, Sarah needed a place to rebuild her strength and self-worth.

We'd been friends for years, and it saddened me to see Sarah struggling with the end of another relationship. During one of our many conversations about marriage, she confessed, "I wish I could be more like you. You seem content to be alone. For some reason, I feel incomplete without a man in my life."

I shook my head. "Don't confuse fear of failure with contentment. I'm trying to figure out what happened in my first marriage before I attempt another relationship. Honestly, Sarah, I'm afraid to date. What if I end up making the same mistake again?"

The Healing

Sarah could not relate to my line of reasoning. She felt so lonely she began dating her estranged second husband. I suspected she was devising a plan to win him back. Even after I shared with her how my three failed reconciliation attempts had led to nothing but more pain, Sarah remained determined to make her second marriage healthy again.

We were both cut from the same cloth. Our cords of codependency bound us to the lies we told ourselves. We convinced ourselves we could fix our ailing marriages. The need to keep our marriages intact was, we believed, the key to our survival. If our marriages dissolved, we feared blame and toxic shame would be the IV drip—a drip, drip, drip that would taunt us forever.

For a codependent, divorce is the worst kind of affliction--failure. A fatal disorder that causes us to bleed to death emotionally. Co-addicts like me are convinced no one else will ever love us again.

To reinforce my walk toward recovery, I chose a path lined with Al-Anon and Christian support groups. This time, my wobbly faith didn't focus on winning. I just wanted to finish. I prayed grace would meet me at the finish line.

And He did.

But those who trust in the LORD will find new strength. They will soar high on wings like eagles. They will run and not grow weary. They will walk and not faint (Isaiah 40:31).

8. Nesting in the Truth

The Journey

Counselors caution people involved in unhealthy relationships or dealing with addictions that a geographical move will not solve their problems. Despite reading about and hearing this warning repeatedly, I had convinced myself my circumstances were different. My plan to move to Florida did not mean I was running away from my problems. I just wanted to be closer to my daughter and grandkids.

Sarah beat me to it. After her efforts to reunite with her second husband failed, she almost-too-quickly became a Miami resident. A fresh start, she told me.

In the meantime, my neighbor Mindy was setting new boundaries. Just home from college and at the end of a toxic relationship she asked if she could move in after Sarah left.

Wise for her years, Mindy mustered the nerve to break up with a boyfriend who failed to treat her with respect. Her confession surprised me. "Nelson wants me to move in with him, but I know that arrangement will never work. I have to learn to live on my own and not get drawn back into another unhealthy situation."

The Healing

After living with three women my age, God sent a young twentysomething woman to enlighten me. He would unveil His plans and break down my walls of ignorance. Why should I be surprised? God used many unconventional methods to reach and teach His people.

In the Book of Joshua, the walls of Jericho fell after the Israelites marched around the city seven times and then shouted as loud as they could (6:15, 20).

In the New Testament, Jesus tells His followers seven times is not His formula for forgiving someone who wronged you. "'No, not seven times,' Jesus replied, 'but seventy times seven!'" (Matthew18:22).

My friends and I also faced complex trials and unlikely foes— our spouses. These men had once promised to love us for better or for worse, through sickness and in health. Instead, they had left us. Did God expect us to forgive them?

After numerous meetings with divorce attorneys and visits to the domestic relations office to settle child support, I discovered I did not have the stamina to continue to drag my resentment along. Maybe Jesus was onto something in His seventy times seven principle. Could He have meant it would be healthier for me if I forgave—sooner rather than later?

In time, Bernice forgave her husband for forcing her to temporary leave the family home. And when Ellen realized the folly of fighting over the penny jar, she let bygones be bygones and returned the container of coins to her husband. Sarah, with her forgiving spirit intact, reached out and bid an amicable goodbye to both of her ex-husbands.

I worked on softening my negative judgments against Bob. In my search for answers about the insidious nature of alcoholism, I found compassion and tolerance. There were times when a certain song, a rerun of our favorite movie, the scent of his brand of aftershave stirred up memories in me—both sweet and bitter. Still, I worked at letting the resentment go.

Thank God for Mindy, the youngest sojourner, who taught me to respect myself and stand firm in the face of adversity. Moving to another city would not change my inner condition. Regardless of where I lived, when I exercised the power of the Holy Spirit, the doors of my heart would open and forgiveness of self and others would enter in.

Don't grieve God. Don't break his heart. His Holy Spirit,

moving and breathing in you, is the most intimate part of your life, making you fit for himself. Don't take such a gift for granted. Make a clean break with all cutting, backbiting, profane talk. Be gentle with one another, sensitive. Forgive one another as quickly and thoroughly as God in Christ forgave you (Ephesians 4:30-32 MSG).

Notes:

Part Four: The Jersey Girls

9. Stranded but Never Alone

The Journey

"Oh no, God, please don't let it break down now," I moaned as my little Dodge Omni sputtered and bucked down the Pennsylvania Turnpike. The Bible story of the hemorrhaging woman immediately came to mind. I had no idea why. That didn't stop me from reminding the Lord, "Jesus, You helped that frightened, lonely woman. Now I'm reaching out to touch Your garment of mercy. Please help me get to the next exit."

After visiting Paul and Jonathan at college, I was deep in the Pocono Mountains, an hour from home. About five miles from the nearest exit, my baby blue car began losing power. I had to keep going. With the grace of God, the car continued to limp along until I reached the tollbooth. Then the engine stopped.

By the time the two turnpike employees pushed my car to the side parking lot, my anxious prayers had turned to bitterness. *Why me, God? Why did this happen to me at night and so far from home?*

Self-pity prompted the blame game. This was all Bob's fault. If we were still together, we would've visited the boys in a reliable car. But no, he bought a new car, moved out, and left me with an old clunker that's spewing smoke in the middle of nowhere!

The Healing

Just when it seemed my life was starting to improve, I had to deal with another setback. I had a secure job and the boys were settled in at college, but now the car died on me. What next?

In Mark's gospel, the woman with the discharge of blood also sought relief. She had spent all she had, only to discover she could not buy healing. She thought, "If I can just touch his robe, I will be healed" (Mark 5:28).

Perhaps her resilience is what brought this narrative to mind when I broke down on that dark, lonely night.

My codependent nature often resorted to blaming and bitterness but never offered peaceful solutions. I knew I had to seek another way. There had to be something, someone, who could make me well again. In desperation, I reached out to touch the Lord's healing robe of mercy, and He responded by touching my heart with hope. My cloak of martyrdom fell away when my Father God led me to a church that practiced His message of unity.

Through prayer and Bible study, I learned we don't have to come trembling from behind. The hem of His garment flows free for all of us to touch. If we extend a finger, our God of Healing will dry up our afflictions and, if we are open, our addictions.

> *Just then a woman who had hemorrhaged for twelve years slipped in from behind and lightly touched his robe. She was thinking to herself, "If I can just put a finger on his robe, I'll get well." Jesus turned—caught her at it. Then he reassured her: "Courage, daughter. You took a risk of faith, and now you're well"* (Matthew 9:20-21 MSG).

10. God's Affirmative Action

The Journey

The small, bleak turnpike office offered little comfort as I waited for road service. In the same room, two African-American women sat and waited. They also appeared distressed.

Before long, I noticed that while the turnpike staff treated me kindly, their body language communicated a subtle hostility toward the other two travelers. In fact, just the presence of the black women seemed to irritate the turnpike employees.

I wondered if these women were in the same situation I was in. I asked them, "What happened? Did your car break down too?"

They took turns explaining. "We left Camden this morning to visit relatives in North Jersey, but we had trouble reading the map and somehow ended up on the Pennsylvania Turnpike."

They drove most of the day, spent their money on lunch, gas, and tolls. Eventually, they ran out of gas and had no money left for the tolls.

"What are you going to do? How will you get home?"

"A couple hours ago, we called our cousin in New Jersey. He's supposed to bring us some money."

"What! A couple of hours ago and you're still sitting here?" In my typical take-charge manner I prompted, "If I were you, I would call again."

Apprehensive at first, one of the women asked the turnpike official if she could make another collect call to her cousin.

It was unmistakable. The employee's response to this woman's request was markedly different from when I had asked to make a phone call. Frowning, the employee handed the woman the phone, saying curtly, "Make it quick."

The Healing

Until I met the Jersey girls, I had tricked myself into believing I was the only legitimate victim in the spectacle that was my life. This night, I saw things differently. As a white woman, I could never relate to their predicament or understand their struggles. Immobilized, like watching the school bully picking on the smallest girl in class, I stood by and watched the injustice. Hopelessness engulfed my Camden friend's round face when she reached her cousin only to learn he had not yet left New Jersey.

Was this kind of non-response typical of what these women had come to expect? Had years of stabbing remarks and curt gestures crushed their self-esteem? Luke 8:43 tells us the woman with the issue of blood "had spent every penny she had on doctors but not one had been able to help her." These tired women from a neighboring state had spent all their money and called their relatives, yet no one was on their way to rescue them.

My thoughts drifted to the reality of the situation. *You think you're in a bad situation, Diane. You may be alone, but others treat you with respect. You know how to read a map. You have the benefit of a towing service. You have people you can rely on. If you had called your sons, sister, or cousins, they would have rushed to help you. You have a credit card for goodness sake.*

The events of that night revealed how not everyone enjoys that kind of assurance and hope. As individuals and as a society, how long will we speak of fairness but continue to demean others and thereby degrade ourselves? Whenever we judge others are not equal to us, we segregate ourselves from the Great Physician's healing power.

Regardless of our skin color, our Creator God will heal our physical and emotional breakdowns. With kindness in our hearts, each deliberate step we take toward Him will purge the prejudiced condition from our souls. With God, our healer, we will get better.

She had suffered a great deal under the care of many doctors and had spent all she had, yet instead of getting better she grew worse. When she heard about Jesus, she came up behind him in the crowd and touched his cloak, because she thought, "If I just touch his clothes, I will be healed." Immediately her bleeding stopped and she felt in her body that she was freed from her suffering (Mark 5:26–29 NIV).

Notes:

11. God's Perfect Solution—A GPS You Can Count On

The Journey

There were no magazines to read, no television to watch. The noisy static from the police radio added to my anxiety. Three women— hostages in a turnpike office. To suppress my paranoia, I began to practice an attitude of gratitude. Lord, You touched me! I was driving alone in a broken down car and You presented Your plan.

In a spirit of meditation, I continued. *Tonight's misfortune is not about me, is it, Lord? Tonight is a reminder of all the times Your power has blessed me. Whenever I reached out, You never turned to see if I was skinny, fat, short, or tall. You never asked my religion, nationality, or race. You never made me check an application form stating whether I was single, married, widowed, or divorced. Without prejudice, You saw me through Your color-blind eyes of love.*

The Healing

Tears of understanding swelled up, threatening to spill over. I knew what I had to do. I would follow my Father God's example and come to the aid of His two daughters, my Camden sisters in Christ. Filled with a spiritual sense of guardianship, I knew I had to help.

My mind shifted into overdrive. *What little cash I have in my wallet can cover the tip for the tow-truck driver. And I have money in my Sunday offering envelope right here in my purse.* I opened my bag, handed my weekly church envelope to the women, and told them to use the money to buy gas for their trip home.

Next, I grabbed a complimentary map from the office wall rack, showed the women where we were, and highlighted the route to New Jersey. "If my car were operational, I would drive to Camden and you could follow me." I chuckled to myself. *Yes, but if my car didn't overheat, our paths would have never crossed.*

At last, the tow truck arrived. As the driver hitched up my car, I slid into the cab of his truck. We drove into the cold night. I never found out if the women waited for their cousin to guide them home or if they found the courage to journey on their own. But this was not about *me*. It was about my response to God's call to action.

The women from Camden and I did have something in common. I also used to believe I had to persevere through life's trials. I was reluctant to ask God and others for help. Fellowship in a Bible-based church would change all that. By their example, my church friends displayed an ongoing assurance in a charitable Father God. I came to understand that asking for help was not a sign of weakness, but one of commendable confidence in a Power greater than myself.

Regardless of the time of day, the weather, or location, I can rely on my internal GPS—God's Perfect Solution. From His unobstructed view of the universe, He directs my trip from start to finish. Even if it means facing a detour, or taking a long way around, I know He will always see me safely home. Father, I pray you will give all Your children the courage to step boldly before You and ask Your direction for the remainder of life's journey.

> *"I will search for my lost ones who strayed away, and I will bring them safely home again. I will bandage the injured and strengthen the weak..."* (Ezekiel 34:16).

12. Sisters, Brothers, All

The Journey

Blinding starbursts from the headlights of oncoming traffic made me grateful I was not driving. During the quiet ride in the tow truck, I questioned how a routine ninety-minute trip had evolved into a tiring four-hour ordeal.

Tiny and tattered, I pulled my pocket New Testament from the bottom of my purse. Leaning toward the dashboard lights, I struggled to read the story of the hemorrhaging woman in Mark's Gospel. For the first time, I noticed this well-known Scripture story began with Jairus, a leader of the local synagogue, begging the Teacher to heal his young daughter. Distinguished leader or not, Jairus was forced to wait while Jesus stopped to talk with the afflicted woman.

Our Lord knew a little girl lay dying, but without so much as a pivot He was aware another daughter had waited years for her healing moment. In His divine providence, Jesus brought these two daughters together in the same moment in time. One born twelve years earlier, and one who had waited for healing during those same twelve draining years. And He blessed them both.

I marveled. Jesus, You were sidetracked too! You were on your way to heal the daughter of a synagogue leader when a poor, bleeding woman sought your healing touch. Neither their age nor their station in life weighed into your equation. You took the time to care for both.

The Healing

The events that night literally brought me to a screeching halt. The experience showed me how others were hurting too. I am not a patient person, but I'd had to wait for the mechanic to pick me up. He had chosen to close his garage at the usual time before arriving in his tow truck to drive me and my car home. The delay forced me to witness how two weary African-American women acted in their distress, and how others, including myself, reacted to their plight.

As the truck passed each mile marker, I silently asked the Healer, *Jesus, was that Your intent when You safely guided me to the turnpike exit? You wanted me to meet the Jersey girls. You brought these two sets of daughters—the two from Camden and the other from Pennsylvania— together in the same moment in time. And You blessed us.*

Now when I pray to overcome my bigotry and shortcomings, I also pray others will hear God's message of harmony. The bleeding woman had to act while Jesus was near, and I could wait no longer to forgive. It was not easy, but being sidetracked helped me see the need for Christ-like compassion toward minorities, the disabled, and the addicted—including my estranged alcoholic husband.

Prayers and Scripture reading paid off. God's Word motivated me to continue my study and to work with those suffering from addictions. Doing so accelerated my own recovery and helped me to recognize the difference between compassionate caring and obsessive enabling.

Father God, help me accept Your message of unity. Build my character. Teach me to apply sincere, personal counsel to those in need.

That's exactly what Jesus did. He didn't make it easy for himself by avoiding people's troubles, but waded right in and helped out. "I took on the troubles of the troubled" ...God wants the combination of his steady, constant calling and warm, personal counsel in Scripture to come to characterize us, keeping us alert for whatever he will do next (Romans 15:3-4 MSG).

13. Never a Bother

The Journey

"Mom, I hate to bother you, but I was wondering if I could use your car. Mine is in the garage, and I can't afford to take time off from work."

Who would have guessed it would come to this. A middle-aged woman turning to her mother for help. I had to. My insurance didn't cover a rental car while mine was in the shop. I knew my seventy-five-year-old mother would not refuse to help me, but it embarrassed me to have to ask. I didn't like relying on others and I didn't want to inconvenience her. I willingly helped others, yet my lack of self-worth often prevented me from asking for assistance.

Of course, my mother loaned me her car. She was happy to help. This was my hangup, not hers.

Because of my co-addiction and compulsive issues, I imagined others saw me as I saw myself—a nuisance.

Well-meaning friends had tried to reassure me. "You'll be fine. You don't need counseling; there's nothing wrong with you." How wrong they were.

Three decades of marriage dominated by dysfunction had changed me. I often looked for but had yet to find the bubbly, outgoing person who used to live inside my hardening shell. With my energy depleted, any hope for a happy, secure future had drained away. After years of hemorrhaging my common sense, I hardly recognized myself anymore.

I needed help.

Scripture reveals many intimate stories of people seeking help. Like the father of the twelve-year-old who had petitioned Jesus. And the grown woman with the continuous flow of blood who risked public humiliation to seek Jesus' healing touch. Neither was any trouble to the Teacher.

In an office on the Pennsylvania turnpike, three women from different backgrounds met by chance, and one discovered they shared a sisterhood dating back to the beginning of time. As if these three women had been His only child, our Father God heard their unspoken cries.

And He came to our rescue.

The Healing

"Hi. My name is Diane, and I am a codependent."

It wasn't easy going to an Al-Anon meeting and admitting I needed help. I was as enthusiastic about a 12 Step meeting as I was about going to the gym. I did not want to go. Once I got there I was fine. I always felt better about myself after I left the meeting—and the gym. Support groups helped redefined my goals. Only after I identified and admitted I had weakness did I find my spiritual strength.

The state-accredited addiction counseling courses I enrolled in at Bucks County Community College prepared me for a position at a drug and alcohol center. Working with addicts and HIV patients taught me how the miracle is not in reaching out to touch our Savior's clothing. The real miracle comes when we believe *His* touch can change our lives.

Overwhelmed by His accessibility, I now know that I am not troubling the Teacher when I ask for Godly wisdom. These were the lessons He died to disclose. Regardless of my age, I am still His little girl. You too are His little girl. You are His little boy.

We are His only child.

While he was still speaking to her, messengers arrived from the home of Jairus, the leader of the synagogue. They told him, "Your daughter is dead. There's no use troubling the Teacher now." The crowd laughed at him. But he made them all leave, and he took the girl's father and mother and his three disciples into the room where the girl was lying. Holding her hand, he said to her, "Talitha koum," which means "Little girl, get up!" And the girl, who was twelve years old, immediately stood up and walked around! They were overwhelmed and totally amazed (Mark 5:35, 40-42).

Notes:

Part Five: Answering the Call

14. How Far Will You Go?

The Journey

This cannot be good. It's almost 9:30 at night. Unless it's an emergency, my family and friends know never to call me after 9:00 PM.

"This is Barbara," she sobbed. "A mutual friend told me to call you because you're a Christian. I don't know who else to call. I need your help."

I didn't recognize the voice. But could it be *that* Barbara? My ex's current flame?

I sucked in my breath. Why would she call me?

Knees wobbling, I leaned against the kitchen wall and slowly slid to the floor. The late night caller had rendered me speechless. Sitting on the cold hardwood floor, I listened as my estranged husband's girlfriend shared her anguish.

I had never met this woman, but I knew her pain.

Through sobs, she described that pain. "I need you to help me let go of my Robert. I need you to help me stop loving him."

Her Robert?

She meant *my* Bob. She couldn't have known those had been my goals, too. Why didn't "her Robert" tell her I hadn't let go of him? He had left me.

It had been five years since my husband and I had separated, but neither of us was in a hurry to finalize our divorce. Bob had navigated through several female friends, and now his new girlfriend was calling me, desperate to let him go. How could I help a stranger deal with issues I had not yet fully resolved?

Ring Around the Rosie was one of my favorite childhood games. With my eyes closed, I held my friends' hands as we giggled and twirled around and around in a circle. When we all fell down, I opened my eyes to see the smiling faces of my friends. Sitting on a cold kitchen floor listening to a stranger describe her troubled relationship with my husband was not a game. My head was spinning, but no one was smiling. With my eyes wide open, I worried how I could help Barbara and, at the same time, keep the steady balance I found in 12 Step meetings.

Barbara continued to share what was to me an all too familiar story. The rescuer in me wanted to believe her. But, could I trust her, or had she used the Christian card to manipulate me into helping her?

No one would blame me if I hung up on her.

Christian or not, what could the woman possibly expect of me? I was still the wife in this drama. Each day I trod water to keep from drowning in my own torment, and she wanted me to save her? Just what did Barbara think being a Christian meant?

What did *I* think it meant?

Cold air from the damp basement seeped up through the floorboards, causing my voice to quiver. Or was my nervousness betraying me? Hugging my bathrobe tighter to stop from shivering, I propped the phone on my shoulder and prayed. *Lord, just because I profess to follow You, do I have to help this woman—the rival for my husband's affections?*

In the middle of this prayer, my martyrdom mentality surfaced. Really, Lord, why is it always up to me to fix other people's problems?

The Healing

My spirit answered. *You know the symptoms of the disease of co-addiction. You've been through the depression, the isolation, the self-loathing that comes from the need for approval. You can do something. You can offer this woman hope.*

My left hand leaned on the floor and I pushed myself up. Then I spoke up. "Barbara, this is awkward. I'm not sure I'm the person you should be asking for help. I don't know what I could do to change how you feel about Bob."

"You know him," she cried. "I hoped you could tell me what I could do to help him."

Ah, there it was—the unvarnished truth. Barbara wanted to help him when her focus should have been on helping herself. She was a fellow codependent. She put her need to fix the addict in her life before her own recovery. If she failed in changing Bob, shame and blame would be her daily companions. She was not interested in getting over "her Robert." She wanted tips on how to fix him.

If Barbara was like me, like most enablers, she convinced herself her efforts to fix Bob would make him love her more. Until she was ready to admit she was powerless to change him, she was in her own self-imposed prison.

Maybe I was the right person to talk with. When I had reached out for support, I needed to know I would not die in my despair. I wanted to believe I would laugh again. With the help of friends and support groups, I was getting better. It was my turn to do for Barbara what others had done for me.

It was time I put Step 12 into practice: Having had a spiritual awakening as the result of these steps, we tried to carry this message to others and to practice these principles in all our affairs.

When I was hungry, you gave me something to eat, and when I was thirsty, you gave me something to drink. When I was a stranger, you welcomed me, and when I was naked, you gave me clothes to wear. When I was sick, you took care of me, and when I was in jail, you visited me." Then the ones who pleased the Lord will ask, "When did we give you something to eat or drink? When did we welcome you as a stranger or give you clothes to wear or visit you while you were sick or in jail?" The king will answer, "Whenever you did it for any of my people, no matter how unimportant they seemed, you did it for me" (Matthew 25:35-40 CEV).

15. A Higher Power Who Makes House Calls

The Journey

If I were honest, I would have to admit I used to stalk Barbara and Bob.

It all began when I first learned about my estranged husband's girlfriend. I badgered old friends until I found someone to tell me who his new sweetheart was. I got her name and address, then drove past her house every weekend to see if Bob's car was parked in her driveway.

Back then, I'd been that reckless. That desperate. Fortunately, time had healed my wounds. Somewhat.

Now I found myself talking with and praying for the woman I'd once stalked. The gravity of Barbara's plea disturbed me. In her, I saw myself. Her all-too-familiar saga echoed my own story. Although we were strangers, we shared a bond that extended beyond our love for the same man. We both exhibited the same compulsive caretaking behaviors.

Raw, detailed feelings poured from Barbara's soul. The more she shared, the more I knew I wanted to help her. However, I still held to the belief that Bob would someday stop drinking and come home. Like the Good Samaritan encountering his adversary, I was being asked by God to help another of His dejected daughters. My inner spirit prompted me to heed His call.

Your encouragement can be the anointing oil that will give her the confidence to move out of this entangled relationship. Your example can be the healing balm that soothes her wounded spirit.

The Healing

From deep within, I found the words I needed to say. "Barbara, would you like to get together and talk?"

Without hesitation, she agreed to meet.

I won't lie. I was dying to see what she looked like. If this Barbara were a size two Barbie doll, then it would be time to stop believing Bob would ever come home to me. Or maybe she wasn't at all like that, nothing like the gorgeous model I was imagining. I hoped meeting her would dissolve the taunting images in my mind.

"Let's meet next week at the Crossroads Inn. It's at the other end of the county, and no one will recognize us there."

"Thanks, Diane. I would like that."

In one trembling motion, my forehead leaned against the flowered wallpaper, as my sweaty palm ended the most bizarre call I had ever received. It was my turn to cry. Few tears fell before my thoughts turned back to Barbara. How desperate she had to be to call me, the wife-in-limbo. The reality was, Barbara had my number before she looked it up in the phone book. We were so alike. She must have figured she could count on my willingness to help. Codependents will go to great lengths to help the addicts in our lives. But why does it always have to be at the expense of our own respectability?

Self-destructive enabling had left emotional scars. My fixation on my spouse stripped away my self-esteem. Despite my rocky road trip, the Great Physician did not pass me by. He heard my cries for help, and thanks to 12 Step support groups my blistering wounds began to heal. My Higher Power revealed an emotional, physical, and spiritual awakening was possible for everyone. Barbara and I included. And He even made house calls.

> "...A Jewish man was traveling on a trip from Jerusalem to Jericho, and he was attacked by bandits. They stripped him of his clothes, beat him up, and left him half dead beside the road. By chance a priest came along. But when he saw the man lying there, he crossed to the other side of the road and passed him by. A Temple assistant

walked over and looked at him lying there, but he also passed by on the other side. Then a despised Samaritan came along, and when he saw the man, he felt compassion for him. Going over to him, the Samaritan soothed his wounds with olive oil and wine and bandaged them. Then he put the man on his own donkey and took him to an inn, where he took care of him" (Luke 10:30-34).

Notes:

16. Breath of Life

The Journey

Faded hex signs on weather-beaten barns overshadowed the new housing developments. Century-old stone farmhouses and milking sheds spread out in fields next to streets saturated with vinyl-sided two-story homes. On my way to meet Barbara, I passed historic town taverns known for their hospitality. They now welcomed the long-time neighbors and new residents alike. Did Barbara expect me to welcome her into my heart house?

Would I?

Could I?

Since I used to frequent the local bar with Bob, I knew most of the people living in the area. However, I had never crossed paths with Barbara. This made me think she didn't hang out in bars. Not until she met Bob.

The car radio competed with the plan formulating in my head. I thought about the pre-flight instructions that always made me snicker whenever I traveled. "In the event of an emergency, an oxygen mask will drop. Remember to apply the mask to yourself before assisting others." Every time I heard a flight attendant make that announcement, it felt as if she were talking directly to me. As a codependent, I had an exaggerated sense of responsibility. The standard pre-flight announcement warned me to take care of myself first before attending to the needs of others.

Contented dairy cows filled the bucolic countryside. Would my life ever be that tranquil or am I destined to live a life full of daily drama? Right then I decided if I wanted to help anyone, I would have to first value and protect my own feelings. In my need for perfection and approval, I often scrambled to help others without taking the time to come up for air. I couldn't do that today. Not with Barbara. In my mind,

I created a kind of mantra: "Take care of you first. Do what you can, then detach with love."

I backed into a parking space near the front door of the restaurant in case I needed a quick exit. After I entered the pub, and my eyes adjusted to the dim light, I spotted a woman sitting alone in a booth in the back. One measured step at a time, I made my way toward her. As soon as she saw me, she jumped up to greet me. Without hesitation, without a word, we hugged. This was the first outward sign of how well we understood one another.

Politeness joined our party, and we motioned to each other to sit down first. Seated across from each other I stared at her taking her in. Although she had long blonde hair she was not a Barbie doll, but a mature woman who loved someone who drank too much. As she began to speak, I recognized another trait we both shared—she talked honestly and without reservation.

"I really thought I could change Robert. I was sure he would stop going to the bars with his drinking buddies once he saw how much I loved him and how well I took care of him. Instead, I began joining him." She sighed, her delicate face drawn. "My sisters are upset with my barhopping. They claim I've deferred my self-respect to a man they don't even know. They're pleading with me to end the relationship."

The Healing

As perverse as it sounds, I found it strangely comforting to know I was not the only one caught in the subtle snare of substance abuse. I was tempted to go into control mode and tell her to heed her sisters' advice and run from the dead-end affair. But I stopped myself. Barbara would have to come to that conclusion on her own.

Instead, I let her talk. When it was time for me to share, I told her how I learned the hard way that joining an addict in his or her habit is not an act of compassion. It's just another sick way to prolong the abuse. To encourage her soul searching, I suggested several books on addiction and codependency. I emphasized the value of Al-Anon meetings and recommended the singles group at my church.

When lunch arrived, I'm not sure what was harder to digest, the creamy Amish corn soup or our brittle conversation.

Before the coffee had a chance to cool, Bob's care-giving girlfriend disclosed another stunner. "You may not know this, but after the intervention you and your family held for Bob, he went to a bar. After a few drinks, he drove to my house. He said he knew what you were trying to do, to shock him into going to rehab. Diane, he could not stop shaking. Even though I held him tight, it didn't stop his body from vibrating. Nothing seemed to comfort him."

Barbara's admission made me suspicious. After all I had done to arrange the family intervention, was she the reason Bob walked out? He must have known he could count on her to console him. To enable him. And allow him to keep drinking.

Resentment began to build in my mind. I had to struggle to keep control and prevent negative thoughts from overtaking me. The pains of the past served no purpose now. I had to keep looking forward. I had to take care of myself.

Our lunch meeting ended with my sincere promise. "Barbara, I'll be praying for you."

Peace of mind escorted me to the car. My prayers had worked. I had applied the oxygen mask to myself first, then breathed in the Words of Life and shared them with Barbara. After telling her how God was working in my life, I'd detached with love. It would be up to her to inhale the promises He had in store for her.

Recently, I befriended Barbara on Facebook. Her social media page disclosed she had moved to another state. My prayer is that she has a special man in her life who will love and treat her the way a child of the Almighty deserves to be treated.

"I speak with all sincerity; I speak the truth. For the Spirit of God has made me, and the breath of the Almighty gives me life" (Job 33:3-4).

Postscript.

Weeks later, I received a Hallmark thank you card from Barbara. The following is the word-for-word letter I sent to her in response.

Dear Barbara, received your card yesterday and was glad you wrote. As you said, our hearts have been hurt. And I'll add broken—but repairable.

I have learned so much these last five years since Bob left, but by far the most important was why I behaved the way I did for so many years. I have read every book I could get my hands on dealing with codependency or co-alcoholic. It taught me that I was as dependent on "fixing" or "needing" Bob as he was dependent on alcohol. He couldn't do without a drink, and I couldn't do without him.

It got to the point that he could not stop drinking once he had that 1st drink and it was destroying him. I, too, couldn't stop loving him, taking care of him, or thinking I could cure him—and it was destroying me. That's when I knew I needed professional help. I went to counseling and Al-Anon meetings. What really helped me get it all together was knowing God loved me so much that He didn't want me to be treated or emotionally abused the way I was allowing myself to be abused!

I had to make a choice (or Bob made it by leaving). I was

devastated, but with the help I mentioned I gradually got better. My self-image has improved. Like the person who gives up alcohol, my struggle is a day at a time because the scars or pain are so deep, it still hurts. Just like the alcoholic, I had to stop a lifestyle that was killing me.

My prayers for you are that you will make the decision to love yourself enough to stop taking any kind of mental abuse from any man—or women. I've learned I can't control anyone but myself, and even at that, I was falling short.

With God's help, I am much better. I respect myself because God has a plan for me, and for us all. Certainly, He wants the best for us—so why wouldn't we want what's best for us too!

The book (and it's a paperback) "Women Who Love Too Much" is excellent. It was like my Bible. Please for your own sake, give it a try. My heart hurts because you sound like Diane Jellen did before she slowly started working on herself and got better. Barbara, I know your pain, I know what it feels like to love Bob. And love shouldn't hurt.

Diane

Notes:

Part Six: Stepping Up with Confidence

17. Going Down or Going Up

The Journey

How did I end up here? No windows, no lights. Nothing that promised a bright tomorrow. I was stuck in the dingy stairwell outside my divorce attorney's office. Our chilled exchange echoed in the cramped space.

He spoke first. "What do you think you'll need weekly?"

Weekly, weekly.

His words ricocheted off the concrete walls, repeating in my head. With shaking fingers, I snapped open my faux leather purse and pulled out a folded sheet of notebook paper. Columns of scribbled numbers itemized my financial needs. Mortgage payment. Groceries. Lunch money. Electric bill. Heating bill. Transportation. Clothing. Doctor bills. School expenses.

He took the sheet of paper and shoved the push-bar on the heavy door to go back inside. Then he turned and said, "Wait here."

Here, here.

I stood there, humiliated, shivering in a light coat.

Within minutes he was back, bringing his echo with him. "Would you settle for less?"

Less, less.

He paused, waiting for my response. "What's your bottom line?"

Line, line.

His questions hit the cement walls like a jackhammer tearing up a sidewalk. Then it hit me. Why was *I* always the one who gave in? Because there was no one else, that's why. No one else had done this to me. I had done it to me. My codependent attitude of always settling for less had created the situation I was in. My acceptance of fourth-class citizenry was so obvious my divorce lawyer thought it okay to haggle with me in an unheated stairwell.

Suddenly, I was angry. "Just who do you represent, Mr. Willis?

If it's your job to get me the best possible settlement, why am I standing at the bottom of a stairway while my estranged husband and his attorney are sitting in a comfortable conference room?"

Room, room, room.

The echoing sound of my loud voice boosted my confidence. My first act of liberation—standing up for myself.

It felt good.

The Healing

Like bubble gum stuck to the bottom of a shoe, enabling behavior had clung to the females in my family for generations. Messy entanglement latched on at an early age. As a child, I could sense the tension between my parents. The shouting. The whispers. The tears. I was too young to give it a name, and I doubt my mother knew what she was living with was called denial.

"Shush," Mom would warn, finger to her lips, motioning me to be quiet. "Everything's okay."

As a child, I sensed her words didn't connect with her actions. Nothing was okay in our family. Someone had to make Mom happy again. Someone had to stick up for my dad. Someone had to fix both of them. As the middle child yearning for positive attention, I set out to liberate my family. Then they would notice me and I would be their favorite.

In high school, I was the girl who always told her friends, "No, that outfit doesn't make you look fat." As their personal cheerleader, I was there to soothe them when they were hurt or worried. A shoulder to cry on when they broke up with their boyfriend. I wanted to be popular. I wanted to be everyone's favorite.

Then I met Bob. Wow. He was handsome, athletic, and popular. I felt unfocused at school until I spotted him coming out of homeroom, then my fluttering heart confirmed the truth: I was in love. I had to get Bob to like me. Years of trying to make others notice and appreciate me paid off and, once he got to know me, Bob liked me too. Years later, our marriage vows confirmed I was his favorite.

As Bob's fixer-upper wife, I continued to seek approval by trying to overhaul my husband's shortcomings. My efforts at improving him meant being together as much as possible. Why else would I agree to sit at the corner bar with him weekend after weekend, choking on second-hand smoke?

Just as I had with my family and friends before him, I believed I needed Bob to validate my own existence. Like my mother, I was deep in denial and didn't know it.

It took a humiliating stairway appointment with a divorce attorney to show me how far astray I had allowed my insecurities to lead me. There was nothing wrong with wanting friends to like me. But giving up my dignity because I wanted my lawyer to think I was an agreeable client was too much. The self-realization stirred the angry victim within. The time had come to re-evaluate my motives.

In the lonely stairwell, there were no favorites. No middle child scampering for attention. No best friend cheering on her pal. No wife guarding her beer-drinking spouse. Just two adults playing a game of denial and disrespect. Enough was enough. Time for me to stop allowing others to discount my worth. Actually, it was time I stopped dishonoring myself.

I knew better. I deserved better.

"Mr. Willis, please escort me to the conference room. I am ready to sit down and review my husband's offer for child support."

Dressed in a new suit of confidence, with shoulders back and head held high, I took my place at the table. The men seated around me treated me with the respect I had longed for yet rarely demanded. When I walked out of the lawyer's office that day, I gave myself an imaginary high five. I had negotiated the kind of settlement my family and I needed—and deserved. With each step up the stairway of self-respect, I distanced myself from the complaining enabler I used to be. I discovered how the middle child syndrome played into my codependent behaviors. Recovery groups helped me understand how constantly seeking endorsement failed to cultivate satisfying relationships. Especially in homes where substance abuse lived.

Once I admitted the exact nature of my wrongs to my Higher Power, the misplaced longing for affirmation began to resolve itself. I was done with my old way of life. When all my legal issues were resolved, I promised myself I would move to Florida and start fresh.

> *Don't lie to one another. You're done with that old life. It's like a filthy set of ill-fitting clothes you've stripped off and put in the fire. Now you're dressed in a new wardrobe. Every item of your new way of life is custom-made by the Creator, with his label on it. All the old fashions are now obsolete. Words like Jewish and non-Jewish, religious and irreligious, insider and outsider, uncivilized and uncouth, slave and free, mean nothing. From now on everyone is defined by Christ, everyone is included in Christ (Colossians 3:10-11*MSG).

Part Seven: A Letter Away from Grace

18. Winging It with Grace

The Journey

"Brrr! I'm not trying to rub it in boys, but I can't wait to get to Florida." It was nine degrees out when Paul and Jonathan drove me to the Allentown airport. The arctic weather increased the excitement in our voices as we discussed my plan to buy a house in South Florida. We hugged and said our goodbyes outside the terminal, our breath coming out in bursts of icy vapors.

Inside the terminal, I studied the flight departure monitors. Flight number-Time-Gate-Status. Good. So far, my flight is on time. The smell of warm soft pretzels drew me to the concession stand where I caught up with a mother struggling to say goodbye to her son. He looked like he might be eleven or twelve years old, and he seemed unhappy with his mother's attention. When she fidgeted with his collar and tried to straighten his pullover sweater, he blushed, raising one shoulder in an effort to nudge her away. Without saying a word, he communicated his annoyance. *Stop fussing over me. I'm a grown boy. I can fix my own sweater.*

His silence was my signal to act. I turned my focus from the airport monitors that I could not control and went into a let-me-fix-your-problem mode that I knew I could handle. I approached the woman and introduced myself. She told me their first names, but my mind zeroed in on their last name—Hrace. A feeling of warmth came over me. *You dear soul,* I thought. *You're only one letter away from Grace.*

The mother said her son was going to Texas to spend winter break with his father. She was worried because he would have to change planes in North Carolina.

That was all my need-to-be-helpful heart had to hear. "I'm making a connection in Charlotte, too. When we arrive there, I'd be happy to accompany him to his assigned gate."

In a timid voice, she replied, "If it's not too much trouble. It would ease some of my worry about him being on his own in a large airport."

The boy did his best to act grown up, but his body language betrayed his fears. Parent and child were like two awkward seventh graders at their first dance as they tried to convince each other they were at ease with their new steps toward independence. More heartwarming was the grace of a mother and son who displayed a love and loyalty that miles would not separate.

For now, this mother had to let her son go and trust a stranger to escort him from one airplane to another. She also had to rely on the boy's father to be at the Texas airport to meet him.

Where did this mother find the courage to let her son go?

The Healing

My mind centered on another mother filled with grace—Mary, who had been temporarily separated from her young son, Jesus. After much searching, Mary and her husband Joseph found their twelve-year-old in the Temple. When they saw their son, Mary confessed her anxious days of searching. She could not have known that one day she would have to let her son journey alone again—this time to Calvary, where Jesus trusted His Father would meet Him. Where did Mary find the courage to let her son go?

As a recovering codependent, I still have trouble letting go of unfounded, worried thoughts. Then I remind myself that, regardless of any painful separation my past behaviors may have caused, my God and Guide will never let me go.

It is up to us to let go and let God. When we do, we will discover a God who will always seek after us until we find *Him*. Now, that is Grace.

When they couldn't find him, they went back to Jerusalem to search for him there. Three days later they finally discovered him in the Temple, sitting among the religious teachers, listening to them and asking questions. His parents didn't know what to think. "Son," his mother said to him, "why have you done this to us? Your father and I have been frantic, searching for you everywhere" (Luke 2:45-46, 48).

Notes:

19. Guided by Grace

The Journey

During the flight, my thoughts wavered. One minute, I pictured a playful beach reunion with my daughter and grandkids. The next minute, I recalled the young boy's mother standing at the gate, nervously clutching her woolen scarf and gloves. In my solitude, I saw a breach of family. A father who lived fifteen hundred miles away. A single mother left alone to endure the winter's wrath.

When Bob and I separated, I worried that our high school-aged sons, Paul and Jonathan, would make the decision to move in with their father. Years earlier when our adult children, Kellyann and Rob, left home, I had experienced a temporary sadness. Each time, their absence filled me with a deep sense of loss.

Had I treated Bob as though he were one of my children, too? I wondered. *Had my husband been the "child" I was most afraid of losing?*

The Healing

Young Mr. Hrace sat a few rows behind me on the Charlotte-bound flight. The few times I glanced back at him, he appeared relaxed. Other than his flushed cheeks, he seemed to be handling his first solo flight with flying colors.

At the Charlotte airport, the young boy and I walked the long corridors together. I sensed he was uncomfortable with me beside him. Then I surprised myself and did something I wouldn't normally do.

I let go.

I stopped, pointed up the crowded walkway to his check-in gate in the distance, and allowed him to continue on his own.

Well, I kind of let go. From a safe distance, I followed him to the gate. Every now and then, he would turn back to see if I was still behind him. While he seemed to want to make his way by himself, he also needed reassurance, to know he was not alone. Did he look back in the hope someone was still concerned about him?

Is this how we codependents manage our relationship with our God of Grace? We want the assurance that our Higher Power is always near, but our self-sufficiency orders us to walk ahead and only call on Him when we feel afraid and alone. I was willing to help this young boy get to his destination in the large, busy airport, yet I didn't know how to find the part of myself that was lost in self-doubt.

These days, whenever I reflect on the steps I have traveled, I know that someone was looking out for me too. My Higher Power guided me out of denial's deceit and set me on a straight path to a healthier way of life. Neither I, nor you, nor that young boy should have to keep looking back to see if He is close behind. We have only to listen and follow Him. He is the way.

> *Whether you turn to the right or to the left, your ears will hear a voice behind you, saying, "This is the way; walk in it"* (Isaiah 30:21 NIV).

Part Eight: War in Heavenly Places

20. Travel Armor: More than Just a Carry-on

The Journey

It was worth it. After all my financial wrangling and loan applications, the business trip I was about to take was all about pleasure. Months after my airport encounter with young Mr. Hrace, I boarded another shiny jet to Florida. On my way to sign the papers for the charming cottage I purchased in Lake Worth, there was nothing for this future Floridian to do except sit back and enjoy the flight.

The plane had just leveled off when the flight attendant promised, "We will now begin our beverage service—"

Boom!

A loud explosion over my left shoulder interrupted her announcement.

Screams echoed through the Boeing 737. The lights on the left side of the cabin flickered off, and auxiliary lighting marched into place along the floor.

"Get me off this piece of @#*$#!"

The piercing cry came from the young man across the aisle. His words hung heavy over the rest of the passengers on the Florida-bound aircraft. Well dressed, he appeared to be in his late twenties. One would expect a more controlled reaction to the crisis from someone who looked like a business professional.

"It's a bomb!" screamed the woman next to me.

Her outburst challenged my resolve to remain calm. From my window seat, I could see the wing of the plane. "I don't think so," I stammered. "It sounded like it came from this side of the plane."

Clutching the armrests in a white-knuckled death grip, I fought my own dark thoughts. It couldn't end like this. I have to fulfill my dream of living in the tropics. Was I going to die without telling Kellyann and my sons, one last time, how much I loved them? Without even saying goodbye?

The Healing

My always-be-in-control training told me screaming wouldn't help. Besides, we already had someone in charge of the scream scene. Feelings of helplessness shifted my thoughts to the spiritual surrender I had found in the 12-Step program. Step One, powerless. Step Two, Power greater than myself. Step Three, God as I understood Him.

Years earlier, I had attended a church workshop on the subject of spiritual warfare. Amazed by the power of all methods of prayer, I had found dozens of biblical references to back up this revolutionary type of devotion. One vivid Scripture story told of a war in heaven that ended when Michael and his angels cast out Satan and his fallen cohorts. That particular Scripture may be the reason why, during the in-flight emergency, I prayed that Michael the Archangel would come to our rescue.

My spiritual boldness grew. Deep inside, I believed dying in a plane crash was not part of God's plan for me. So I did what had become natural for me—I whispered a prayer. *Michael, if you really are the great protector of God's people, help us now.* With my eyes squeezed shut, I visualized the Archangel supporting the wounded left side of the plane while an army of angels held up the right.

Startled by a touch, I opened my eyes. The woman next to me clutched my hand in hers, her other hand interlaced with her husband's.

As someone who centered her life on trying to prevent bad things from happening, I now understood the real feeling of powerlessness. Despite the potential disaster, I felt an indescribable peace. I hoped this inner calm would reassure the woman in seat 7B. I turned and reassured her, "It's okay. I'm praying us down."

To prepare myself for whatever was to come, I spiritually

dressed in the unconventional armor St. Paul described in the Book of Ephesians.

> *So put on all the armor that God gives. Then when that evil day comes, you will be able to defend yourself. And when the battle is over, you will still be standing firm. Be ready! Let the truth be like a belt around your waist, and let God's justice protect you like armor Your desire to tell the good news about peace should be like shoes on your feet. Let your faith be like a shield, and you will be able to stop all the flaming arrows of the evil one. Let God's saving power be like a helmet, and for a sword use God's message that comes from the Spirit* (Ephesians 6:13-17 CEV).

A voice from the cockpit captured my full attention. "Ladies and gentlemen. We are experiencing engine trouble and will be returning to the Philadelphia airport."

For a moment, my I-have-a-better-idea mindset resurfaced. We were probably closer to Baltimore Washington International. Why not just land there? I shook my head. Unbelievable. My micromanaging style was trying to tell me I knew more than the pilot did.

Passengers had reacted differently to the threatening situation. The pilot's announcement now provided us with a temporary reprieve. The young man in the business suit, however, ignored the flight attendant's call for calm, continuing to shout and swear. On a plane full of anxious travelers, why was he the only one to react with aggressive outbursts?

Those of us involved in addictive relationships know all about eruptions and upheavals. Holding on to past offenses may feel gratifying, but doing so will not allow the built-up anger to depressurize.

I carried my grudges because they justified the threats I'd made against my husband and, at times, against God. Yet, with each crisis, my faith grew. Through each personal disaster, the 12 Steps, God, and a host of angels in heavenly places were always within my reach.

> *"'That's when Michael, the great angel-prince, champion of your people, will step in. It will be a time of trouble, the worst trouble the world has ever seen. But your people will be saved from the trouble, every last one [whose names are] found written in the Book'"* (Daniel 12:1 MSG).

21. Armor of God: One Size Fits All

The Journey

They were green. Not red. Chartreuse green.

How strange. I had always believed all fire trucks and ambulances were red.

Regardless of color, the battalion of emergency vehicles that lined the runway was a welcome sight. Our crippled plane descended and, while everyone aboard held their breath, the pilot executed a successful landing. Applause filled the cabin as the green fire trucks and ambulances escorted our injured plane to an open gate.

Reclaiming my hand from my fellow passenger, I wiped away the tears of relief, closed my eyes, and reflected.

"I'm next. I'm next," I shouted as I did a cannonball into the frigid lake. Kicking myself back to the surface laughing in unison with my siblings and cousins.

Easter Sunday driving to the 6:00 AM Resurrection Mass with Dziadzi, Mom, Joe, and Peg.

"I do!" Exchanging wedding vows in front of a Justice of the Peace and repeating the same "I do" before a Catholic priest.

These were a few of the life images I thought would flash before me when we were bumping among the clouds. Strangely enough they didn't. Between praying and looking out the window to check the wing for flames, I was thinking about what I was wearing. If the plane caught fire, would my linen pantsuit melt to my skin? This certainly was not the protective spiritual armor of God.

After deplaning, I waited at the top of the jetway ramp for the agitated young man to appear. When he approached, I stepped forward.

"Hi, I'm Diane. You're about the same age as my sons, and I saw how upset you were during this ordeal. It must be my motherly instinct, but I'm wondering if there's anything I can do to help you."

The lanky man with sandy brown hair looked away. "Nah, I'm all right."

Whew. His dry alcohol breath transported me back to any given weekend in our calamity-ridden home. I should have guessed alcohol had played a part in his unruly behavior. Now he was acting humble. How typical.

It took grit for me to rein in my judgmental spirit and listen.

"I'm Brad. I'm okay. I had a couple of drinks before we boarded, which probably didn't help when all hell broke loose up there." He avoided making eye contact as we walked together through the crowded terminal.

"Well, Brad, this may be a good time to get a cup of black coffee and relax until the airline makes arrangements for another plane to Florida."

"Yeah, maybe," was his cool reply. He stretched his neck, looking over my head as if he wished I weren't there.

His body language was my cue to back off. "If you want to talk, I'll be over at the check-in gate."

It was time for me to refocus and call my children.

"Hi, you have reached the ...." Oh no, three of the calls went to voice mail. Finally, Paul picked up. My voice shook as I recounted the near-catastrophic episode in the sky and my spiritual warfare prayers for an assist. Then I asked Paul to contact Kellyann and tell her I would be boarding another flight and would call her when I arrived in Florida.

As I paced past the windows overlooking the tarmac, I recalled Brad's comment about "all hell breaking loose." I thought, *Brad, if you only knew how close Hell was to really breaking loose up there.*

The emergency vehicles had been in place ready to protect our physical bodies. And I believed God and His angels were the spiritual defenders who'd brought us safely back to Philly.

I didn't talk to Brad again, but I continued my heart-to-heart with my Higher Power. *Father God, does this young man's unwillingness to talk to me mirror my reluctance to turn my will and my life over to Your care? Why do I choose to go through life defenseless when I can outfit myself with Your spiritual armor of protection and peace? Show me how to improve my conscious contact with You, and continue to protect me from the battles yet to come.*

My shoes clicked and dragged down the jetway. Fighting fatigue, my mind could not will my legs to step it up. The replacement 737 arrived from Pittsburgh and trancelike passengers funneled into the narrow aisle searching for our assigned seats. For the second time that evening, we left the City of Brotherly Love. When the attendants began the beverage service, I felt somewhat assured we had passed a critical threshold.

A diet Sprite in one hand and my notebook spread out on the tray table, I began to journal. With the events of the aborted flight fresh in my mind, I described how I had enlisted the aid of Michael the Archangel. I wrote about my desire to see my kids again and my prayer that one day they, too, would believe in God's supernatural power. I described the passengers' reactions during the crisis. My journal entry ended with how the remarkable landing confirmed the importance of invoking all types of prayer, including spiritual warfare.

What I did not write was implanted in my memory forever. It was my son Paul's comment. "Mom, they don't realize it, but 200 passengers owe their lives to your prayers."

Was that all God was asking of us—to remain faithful in prayer despite the drama that plays out in our lives? Or are we to gird up our loins in prayer precisely because of the crises we all face at one time or another?

The Healing

Please, God, don't let this be a Groundhog Day flight, my nervous attempt at humor petitioned. Nonetheless, I remained vigilant. Time after time, I looked out the window and gazed down at the black ocean, then stretched to check the dimmed cabin. Each time, reassuring myself everything was normal. This was not a déjà vu flight to Florida.

Two and a half hours later, twinkling lights appeared. The glow was not from heaven's streets of gold. The shining beams were the beachfront city of Fort Lauderdale bidding us hello. Yellow runway lights lined the way as the plane touched down. This time, cheers and applause were replaced by sighs of relief from the weary passengers.

It was 10 PM when I called my kids to tell them I was safe on solid ground. With my purse secure over my shoulder, and pulling my suitcase behind, I waited in line at the car rental counter. Would this day never end? Others in the queue talked about the ordeal we'd all experienced. I chimed in, "I'm just grateful the engine never caught fire."

An older man with a Rocky Balboa South Philly accent shot me a look. "Hey, lady, it's a good thing you weren't sitting where I was. From my window, you would've seen the flames shooting out from the back of the wing."

Flames. Sparks. So Hell *was* breaking loose up there! If I'd seen the fire, I might have reacted like Brad had. Maybe worse.

You were there for me again, Lord, weren't You? I don't always see Your protective hand, but You defend me in more ways than I could ever imagine.

As I thought about what I hadn't seen, my mind turned to my ex-husband. Had my efforts to control him and his addiction failed because my battle was not with him but with his inner demons? If so, only Bob could fight that battle. He would have to cross his own critical threshold and admit he was powerless over alcohol. He would have to trust our God in heavenly places to aid and assist him in overcoming his addiction.

Lord, with Your grace and the wisdom of the 12 Steps, equip us to stand against whatever comes our way. For many, this is a life-or-death fight to the finish. Give us the strength to endure and reign with You one day at a time.

> *And that about wraps it up. God is strong, and he wants you strong. So take everything the Master has set out for you, well-made weapons of the best materials. And put them to use so you will be able to stand up to everything the Devil throws your way. This is no afternoon athletic contest that we'll walk away from and forget about in a couple of hours. This is for keeps, a life-or-death fight to the finish against the Devil and all his angels* (Ephesians 6:10-12 MSG).

Notes:

Part Nine: Non-Stop Train to Paradise

22. Leaving the Baggage Behind

The Journey

This was it! The day had finally arrived. After ten years of praying, planning, and visiting the Sunshine State, I was moving to paradise.

It was only a couple of steps, but I hugged myself to stay warm as I dashed into the heated waiting room of the Amtrak station. Through the three-story wall of windows, I watched an employee drive my red Honda hatchback into the auto-train car carrier. Packed with picture albums, and other personal treasures I didn't want to send via the moving van, my little car with 90,000 miles on the odometer was ready to ride the rails to Florida.

Although it was a gray December day, my outlook was brighter than ever. The auto-train was the final step in my relocation to my new home. Waiting to board in Virginia, I mingled with hundreds of elderly travelers eager to step into the warm sunshine when we detrained the next morning.

My adventurous spirit buoyed me up the narrow stairway to the top level of the train to look for my assigned window seat.

"Wait, let me help you," I offered. Being one of the younger seniors on the train, I found myself guiding an older snowbird by her bony elbow. We carefully swayed our way to our coach seats.

In the dining car, I shared a table with a family on their way to their dream of a lifetime—a week at Disney World. Cheerful commentary from their five-year-old daughter complemented the braised short ribs and salad. Back in my seat, the anticipation of living near my young grandchildren completed my joy-filled day.

Maybe if I turn this way. No, that's not going to work. Maybe leaning on the window and pulling my legs closer. Nope, definitely not comfortable. Unfortunately, it only took one night for my good mood to dissipate. Unable to drift into a deep sleep, after trying to contort my body to fit the supposedly oversized seat, I awoke early. Tired and cranky, I began to journal.

Unexpected feelings of sadness filled up the blank page. I found myself questioning if I had done the right thing in leaving my three adult sons and aging mother in Pennsylvania. Who will take care of them now that I'm no longer nearby?

When the sun broke through the clouds, I looked out the window. Swaying palm trees and fields of bright green ferns dominated the landscape. It was too late to turn around. I was already in Florida. This was home now.

A loud discussion from the couple across the aisle reminded me why I was still single. As I listened, however, I realized their dilemma was far more enlightening than my own diary notes. The secretary in me flipped to a blank page, and I began to record their conversation in shorthand.

"I can assure you of this, they are packed somewhere," the man insisted.

"Where, Harry, where?" the feisty woman beside him asked. "In the yellow bag?"

"I don't know. But I do know they're not at home."

"How do you know that, Harry? How?"

"Because I checked the house before we left. Anyway, the only pills that are important are the ones for my eyes—and these for my heart." He opened his fist. Several colorful capsules decorated his palm.

"I don't want the pills loose, Harry. They should be in a box."

"Put them in your purse."

"No, my purse is dirty."

"Then wrap them in a tissue—one at a time."

They sounded like a couple who'd danced the steps to many anniversary waltzes. When their chatter stopped, a welcome silence filled the fast-moving train.

But not for long.

Harry fretted and fussed. "I don't see my other pills."

"Well, his wife demanded, what makes you think I have them?"

He didn't respond. He continued to rummage through their carry-on bag.

"Harry, they're not in there, I tell you. Stop looking!"

"Okay, but where are the keys to the house?"

"In the Florida bag."

Rattled now, his gruff voice questioned, "Could they be in the other bag?"

When his wife didn't answer, he resorted to his loud playground voice. "What about the Warfarin? Where's the Warfarin?"

"I packed them."

"When? When did you pack them—the second time?"

"What second time?" she quizzed.

"Never mind. Where's the bag?"

"What bag?"

"The white bag—the paper bag."

"On the seat beside me."

"Where? I don't see it. Anyway, don't worry. I could miss a day."

"I'm not worried," she assured him.

"Yes, you are."

"No, I'm not. I never said I was worried. *You* said I was worried, but believe me, Harry, I am *not* worried."

Harry's wife fumbled through her purse. "Somewhere in here is my lipstick."

"Lipstick?" he bellowed. "Maybe it's in the white bag with the Warfarin."

The train's public address system competed with the couple's Seinfeldesque dialogue. Never did I appreciate a static intercom message as much as I did just then. In fact, I welcomed the courtesy announcement.

"Your attention, please. We are an hour ahead of schedule and should arrive in Sanford, Florida, at 8:30 AM."

She was still looking for her lipstick when he hollered, "Are you going to drive?"

"Yes, I'll drive," she said with a sigh.

"No, never mind. I feel good. I'll drive."

"Then why did you ask me if *I* was going to drive?"

Harry pulled out his wallet and shouted, "Do you have any singles?"

"What?"

Ah, it came to me. I understood why they were using their outside voices. They'd forgotten their hearing aids too. Unless they were in the yellow bag with the eye drops?

He repeated, "Do you have any singles?"

"I don't know. Let me look in my purse. No, I only have a five."

Most of the other travelers knew what was coming, and we all fumbled through our wallets looking for five singles. Right on cue, Harry turned to a fellow passenger, "Do you have change for a five dollar bill?"

Two rows back a man's voice barked, "I do."

After a successful financial exchange, Harry said to his wife, "I think the claim number for our car is fifty-nine."

"Yes, it is," she answered.

The train pulled into the station.

Finally, they'd agreed on something.

The Healing

Throughout the trip, Harry had not called his wife by her first name.

You don't suppose he had forgotten her name just like he forgot to pack his pills?

Before I closed my daily journal, I scribbled a final thought: Oy vey! If this is what living in God's waiting room will be like, brace yourself for Florida, Diane. Brace yourself.

The LORD will protect you now and always wherever you go (Psalm 121:8 CEV).

Notes:

Part Ten: Being Frank

23. Waiting for the Right Mate

The Journey

"Who is this?" I asked the man who had called me on the phone. I was bewildered. The voice sounded familiar—a voice from the past. Could it be Frank from Philly?

It had been several years since I'd moved to Florida. I loved my new surroundings and had yet to look back in regret. Every tropical sunrise and color-streaked sunset confirmed my decision to relocate. I was home.

I still kept in touch with many of my friends in Pennsylvania. We talked on the phone often. But when I answered this morning, Frank's voice was the last one I expected to hear.

"It's Frank. I'm going to Disney World with my daughter and her family. I was hoping I could visit you when I'm in Florida."

It was him, all right. Friends had informed me when his wife died six months earlier. While sympathetic to his loss, his request to visit made me uncomfortable. I didn't want him to feel rejected, but I was not going to invite him to stay overnight in my home. That meant setting up clear boundary lines.

The gears in my mind clicked into motion. "So, where will you stay when you're in Palm Beach County?"

"I booked a room at the Hilton a few miles from your place."

He already reserved a hotel room. "Uh, so, well, I guess since you'll be in town, you're welcome to come over for dinner."

An invitation he quickly accepted.

As soon as we hung up, I called my daughter. "Kellyann, I can't believe Frank wants to visit me. Do you think it's appropriate?"

"For goodness sake, Mom, calm down. He's not coming down here to ask you to marry him. He only wants to stop in for a visit."

"Yes, but his wife just died from a heart attack. He should still be mourning."

Kellyann sighed. "Mom, think about it. He's going to be in Florida and doesn't want to be with his daughter and grandkids twenty-four hours a day. He probably sees this side trip as a way to have some adult quiet time."

Still not convinced, I spent the rest of the week cleaning the house. I also planned a simple dinner menu. After all, I didn't want him to think I was auditioning to be his next wife. I agonized about what we had in common that could keep the conversation going while he was here.

The knock on my front door reawakened my feelings of dread. The day had arrived. Frank had actually shown up. He didn't cancel or arrive hours late.

Too bad for me. I'd prayed he wouldn't show.

"Come in," I said to the man on the doorstep. "It's so good to see you, Frank," I fibbed.

His face was more wrinkled than I remembered, and he had lost weight. He looked too thin, stressed. In the living room, we shared a quick, friendly hug. I fixed him a glass of lemonade, then we left to view the sights on Palm Beach Island. After that, we drove along the coast to Jupiter Inlet. My plan was to serve an early dinner so my guest wouldn't linger late into the night.

Back at the house, I busied myself in the kitchen. My guest sat at the table and, without prompting, began to share his grief.

"I told my daughter I cannot live by myself another day. I miss Helen so much. I can't stand being alone," he admitted. "I think about her all the time. I find myself looking for her in every room, waiting for her to come home from work. It's just too painful living in a big empty house with no one to talk to. It's bad enough during the day, but not having anyone to share my nights with is more than I can bear."

My eyes widened. Okay, this was getting way too personal.

What did he expect me to say?

I didn't respond. Instead, I continued to stir-fry the vegetables that would complement the baked salmon. Sure, it was sad Frank was all alone, but I couldn't be a helpful neighbor. I lived 1200 miles away.

Frank stared out the French doors and appeared to be deep in thought. In slow motion, he turned to look at me. "I've met with several single women from work, but none of them were compatible. Diane, do you know how difficult it is to meet someone with the same values and beliefs we share?"

Uh oh.

I swallowed hard. This felt to me like a dating service interview. Did he want me to compare and see if we were suitable for the long haul? See if we were a match?

"Frank, you've suffered a great loss. You and Helen were married a long time, and you've only been alone six months. Don't you think it's too soon to look for someone to take her place?"

I hoped my words would reassure him. When he said nothing, I added, "Most counselors recommend waiting at least a year before making any major life-changing decisions. Have you thought about calling the American Heart Association for a local grief support group? That may help you cope with your loss."

The Healing

Tears began to fall, and Frank's spirit headed in the same direction. We talked about the emptiness that accompanies the loss of a spouse.

I was quick to mention how we all frantically look for replacements. And how rarely that works out.

"To be honest, Frank, after my husband and I separated, I joined a singles group. Like thousands of hurting singles, I wanted someone to take away my loneliness. But no one had the qualifications I was seeking. I was so broken I could have rushed into *any* relationship, but I didn't. I credit my guardian angel for keeping me from making a major mistake."

He nodded, as if encouraging me to continue.

"I did date someone for several weeks, but when he wanted to take our friendship to a more intimate level, I ended it. I was looking for a friend, and he was looking for a lover. I wasn't ready, but I was secure enough to walk away before either of us were hurt."

I looked Frank in the eye and said, "My friend, you need time to heal."

He must have decoded my masked message. After a quiet dinner, he was ready to say good night. Before he left, however, he asked if he could take me to church and breakfast the next morning. I interpreted his request as closure, so I agreed.

In bed, I fretted for what seemed like hours. Twisting and turning, pulling the lightweight quilt on, then kicking it off. I couldn't sleep. I replayed the events of the day in my head. *Frank, I thought you were a trusting, patient man. Why would you, of all people, try to rush God's plan for your future?*

It was foolish to believe I could preach patience to Frank, or anyone else. What little patience I had myself was tested daily. I always seemed to pick the slowest line at the checkout counter or pulled into the snail lane at the thruway tollbooth. I had to force myself not to lose patience.

Support groups advocate trusting in a Higher Power. Their encouragement helped me deal with my codependent need to have immediate answers. Like other enablers, I operated on the belief if I acted quickly and fixed all wrongs, I would gain the personal approval I sought. My accomplishments would earn me the admiration of others.

I have since learned these are myths. The truth is our patient God is never finished with us. He wants to strengthen us in order to reflect a unity of spirit within ourselves. When we say yes to Him, we are never alone.

> *But God's not finished. He is waiting around to be gracious to you. He's gathering strength to show mercy to you. God takes the time to do everything right— everything. Those who wait around for him are the lucky ones* (Isaiah 30:18 MSG).

Notes:

24. Unwilling to Engage

The Journey

There was no doubt. My friend from Philly had an agenda. His visit was more than casual. Frank was leading up to something, and in my heart I knew it.

After a restless night, I readied myself for church, mentally preparing myself in case Frank pressed me. The image looking back from the mirror as I applied "age-defying makeup" convinced me my cover-up foundation was not living up to its promise.

Christian music played on the radio as I slapped the clothes hangers from left to right, looking for the perfect outfit to wear. Talking to myself was one of the benefits of living alone, and my anxiety had me chatting nonstop.

"You know, Diane, if you were going to church alone today, you wouldn't be going through this what-should-I-wear torment."

I answered myself. "I know. It's only Frank, so why am I so uptight?"

The background music faded as my spirit played a stronger message to my heart. *"All you have to do is tell him you are already in a relationship—with Me."*

My instincts were right. God was on my side. He was telling me to be prepared for Frank to pop the big "M" question. No wonder I was nervous. I had been ignoring my spirit. Where else could that reassuring message have come from?

Once again, my date arrived on time. When we got to my church, I led the way inside. My mind, however, was thinking back to the times I went to church with Bob and the kids—as a family. Today, with Frank sitting beside me, I was the one squirming in the pew.

I had been going to church alone for so long, I was startled when my gentleman friend handed me the songbook. My body stiffened when he innocently helped me remove my jacket. During the service, I prayed he would accept a handshake instead of an intimate hug at the sign of peace. I didn't want my friends at church to think we were a couple.

Frank was a man of deep faith who was in great pain. If he was searching for a commitment, I prayed his strong spiritual beliefs would help him understand where I was coming from in refusing his offer.

When the morning service ended, I suggested a nearby restaurant known for their bountiful breakfasts. The server brought coffee, and after she took our order Frank and I sat there looking at each other. It felt unnatural. He didn't speak, so in typical codependent style, I started the conversation. In doing so, I unintentionally gave him a lead-in.

I stirred my coffee. "Did you sleep well?"

He grimaced. "No. I was up most of the night. I was compiling a list of qualities I want in a wife. There is only one person I know who can fill those requirements…"

I closed my eyes. *Oh boy, here it comes.*

"…and that's you, Diane."

The Healing

French toast swimming in syrup and melted butter signaled the butterflies in my stomach to start their fluttering loop-de-loops. I couldn't possibly eat. What had I been thinking when I ordered a big meal?

Pushing my favorite breakfast aside, I reached across the table and looked into his tear-filled eyes. "Frank, I am already in a relationship. I have a spiritual Bridegroom who loves me. He has cared for me and given me all I could ever need. I am content."

His blink released a tear. "I understand, Diane. That's why I made a list of what I'm looking for in a wife. That's why you're the one

I'm asking. I need someone like you to bring God back into my life again."

With a smile, I tried to reassure him. "God is still in your life. You know you can trust Him to fill your emptiness. It's a process that can't be rushed. Give yourself time to feel and work through your grief."

We squeezed each other's hand in unspoken agreement, then let go. The paper napkins on our laps doubled as tissues as we both wiped our tears and tried to force down the first meal of the day.

It was a short, quiet ride back to my house. After a brief embrace, Frank and I said goodbye. He left to join his family in Orlando.

The stress I felt before he arrived and the events leading up to the morning's farewell resurfaced. It was time for my own meltdown.

I paced from the kitchen to the family room. From the family room to the kitchen. Next, I emptied the dishwasher from the night before. Being busy always helped at times of stress. Out in the garden, I pulled weeds and moved potted plants from one spot to another. Then moved them back again.

Feeling fidgety, I decided I had to get out of the house. I needed a change of scenery. A movie would help me unwind. "Excuse me. Excuse me." I said stepping in front of people to claim a seat in the middle of the back row. The weekend's number-one flick was a slow-moving love story. Poor choice. Not surprisingly, I left before the movie ended.

When I arrived home, a floral basket filled with perky daisies and fragile baby's breath decorated the top step of my front porch. The card read, "To Diane, my good friend. Love, Frank."

It was true. Frank needed a friend, not a fiancé.

With a sigh, I thanked God for showing me what to do and say. I was grateful I hadn't relapsed into my old caregiving role. The old me might have agreed to Frank's proposal. Just to help the man. Or I could have been so needy and smitten by his proposal, I accepted. Instead, I followed my deepening spiritual sense of worth.

There would be future propositions to tempt me. And someday, I might say yes to someone. Today was not that day. Today I would rejoice because I had a Bridegroom who gave me the courage to speak words of truth.

> *...Then God will rejoice over you as a bridegroom rejoices over his bride* (Isaiah 62:5).

25. Staying Power

The Journey

My friends chatted about their husbands while I sat there mute.

"Eli picked up hot garlic wings and pepperoni pizza for supper."

"Mike installed new heat-resistant window blinds at the shore house."

"Now that we're retired, Marcus and I both collect Social Security."

As I listened to the conversation, I wondered if my girlfriends realized how lucky they were. Who was going to run out and buy my dinner, help me with household chores, pool their Social Security check with mine?

Nobody. No one at all.

"On my own" was the theme of the pity party I was hosting. Dwindling finances had initiated this party. Like thousands of others, I'd tried to cash in on the booming Florida real estate market. I'd invested in a small condominium that I was planning to flip in order to make a nice little retirement nest egg. Then the bottom fell out of the market. I now owned two houses with plummeting values.

Two monthly mortgage payments were the only companions I could count on.

I had been making solo decisions for years, so when the housing market hit bottom, I knew I had no one to blame but myself. Blame—the classic tormentor of my soul. Where else could I point a finger? I couldn't blame my deceased ex-spouse. It was all on me. I had to take full responsibility.

My job as a school secretary drained me physically and mentally. The demands from the principal, teaching staff, students and parents wore me down. However, I could not retire until I sold one of the two homes and paid off the mortgage.

Jealousy laid a snare for me whenever others described how they shared responsibilities in their marital partnerships. There was only one way to free me from the trap of the green-eyed monster. It was time I met someone instead of spending my golden years alone.

Someone who would help me grocery shop, mow the lawn, and pay the bills.

The Healing

Clearly, I was not looking for someone to love and cherish in sickness and in health. I wanted an energetic errand boy who was also a prudent property manager and gifted financier. Yep, I was sure that's what I needed.

It had been less than a year since Frank's proposal. What had caused my confidence in my spiritual Bridegroom to diminish? If I believed God was with me, why did I think a man could fix my problems?

Storms of doubt had swept in, engulfing me, forcing me to fill the gaps in my life with whitewashed lies and false hopes.

Question after question whipped through my spirit, chipping away at my once strong resolve. In my heart, I knew God loved me too much to let me build a marriage based on financial needs. He loved me too much to let me seek after a relationship that would quickly collapse due to a weak foundation. Moreover, He loved me far too much to let me continue to covet others' marriages.

Just in time—His time—God showed me the foolishness of a whitewashed, quick-fix remedy. All was not lost. Patience won. I survived the storms of lies that beat at me, and I began to rebuild my one home with God.

"...When people build a wall, they're right behind them slapping on whitewash. Tell those who are slapping on the whitewash, 'When a torrent of rain comes and the hailstones crash down and the hurricane sweeps in and the wall collapses, what's the good of the whitewash that you slapped on so liberally, making it look so good?'" (Ezekiel 13:10-12 MSG).

Notes:

Part Eleven: When Being Alone is a Choice

26. Dancing with an Angel

The Journey

A lifetime had passed since the period of anger that followed when my husband and I first separated. Back then, finding a healthy solution was not on my list of self-improvement. Vengeance, however, was. After months of sitting home and feeling sorry for myself, I agreed to join my friend Cheryl at a singles bar. Maybe I'd get lucky and meet a drop-dead gorgeous hunk of a man. That would be a perfect revenge.

I stepped out with a new hairstyle, but I wore my same old revengeful spirit. "Cheryl, if Bob thinks I'm a disposable Bic bride to be used and tossed, he's going to learn just how spiteful I can be. When we go to court, I'm going to fight to get the maximum in alimony payments. Then I'm going to use his hard-earned money to get a facelift."

Cheryl looked at me in surprise. "I understand why you're angry, Diane, but give yourself time to adjust."

"Adjust! I'll show you adjust. During our thirty years together, I danced around Bob's mood swings. I bore that man four kids. I cleaned and cooked." My anger meter was just getting started. "I was his designated driver before the term was ever coined. Then he decides *he* doesn't want to be married anymore. He's going to feel rejection's sting when I renounce our marriage and reclaim my maiden name."

Behind my bravado, I was choking back the tears. Would Bob really care if I found someone else? He'd probably be happy if I changed my name and was no longer connected to him. Would any man want to be with me? Or would I spend the rest of my adult years alone, a bitter old maid?

The singles bar was not like our old high school dances. The crêpe paper streamers and balloons were missing. There were no vinyl records spinning on a record player. The girls were not lined up on one side of the gym, the boys on the other. Instead, Cheryl and I were part of a gaggle of women nursing glasses of white wine in a dark, smoke-filled bar.

Cheryl pointed out the lounge lizards, older men attempting to look younger than their years by dressing casual and sucking in their pouch bellies. In one hand a balancing act with a beer glass, while an elbow leaned on the bar for support.

I talked myself down, trying to remain calm. *Remember, no eye contact. Follow Cheryl's lead, scan the room, and center back to your conversation.*

Too late. A guy with a wrinkled sport coat caught my eye.

Please, God, don't let him ask me to dance. I haven't danced with anyone other than my husband in years. I wouldn't know how to follow someone else's lead. Uh-oh, he's staggering this way. He looks like he's had too much to drink.

Sure enough, the stranger with the bloodshot eyes asked me to dance. I didn't want to, but my need to please won out.

I hadn't lost my touch. I could still attract men—the ones who like to drink too much. When the music stopped, I grabbed my purse, said good night to Cheryl, and whisked out into the fresh night air.

The Healing

Trying to market myself to get a man wasn't going to work. It didn't feel right. I couldn't date someone just to settle the score with Bob. It felt better to trade my dancing shoes for warm fuzzy slippers and reruns of *Law and Order: Special Victim Unit.*

Flicking through the channels, I wondered if spending my evenings alone or going out dancing with emotionally insecure people were the only alternatives open to me. If so, I would have to face—head on—my fear of living alone for the rest of my life.

Alone it was. Weekends were always the most difficult. I no longer sat at the local pub with Bob on Friday and Saturday nights. Now I sat home alone.

When I found a Friday night Al-Anon meeting, my victim temperament began to lose its punch. It was there that I learned to make wise lifestyle choices. Little by little, my manic personality began to change as I welcomed the calm spirit who moved in. The more time I took to get to know the real me, the more I liked myself.

In God's timing, I had a head-in-the-clouds encounter. This happened the year my granddaughter was born. I was still living in Pennsylvania and flew to Florida for Bridget's christening. My estranged husband and his mother also attended. Ann and I had remained friends, so I accepted her invitation to meet at their hotel for a drink the night before the christening. Bob would be there too.

Valet parking always made me feel special and tonight was definitely a valet parking event. Straightening my silky blue pantsuit, fluffing my hair, I tried to leave my poor self-image in the lobby, but she insisted on escorting me into the lounge. I checked my pocket mirror one more time. I had to look perfect.

Ceiling to floor windows framed the moonlit Atlantic Ocean and Ft. Lauderdale's long white beach. I did my best to look sophisticated as I walked to the mahogany bar where two empty bar stools were available, one next to Bob, the other beside Ann.

I sat down next to my mother-in-law.

Ann and I talked about the upcoming baptism and the precious baby girl who had brought us together, albeit temporarily. Bob and his long-time companion, old Mr. Brooding, kept to themselves. Occasionally, I leaned across the long shiny bar to include my estranged husband in our conversation, but his responses seemed gruff. So I stopped trying.

I had finished my glass of wine and was getting ready to leave when a male voice whispered in my ear. "Excuse me, would you like to dance?"

Out of nowhere, a trim, handsome, silver-haired gentleman with a welcoming smile had appeared beside me. And he wanted *me* to join him on the dance floor.

If I said yes, Bob would be upset. I started to say no, then stopped. Wait a minute, I reminded myself, we're separated. Why should I care what Bob thinks?

The well-groomed stranger guided me gracefully across the dance floor, never missing a beat. As if choreographed, the smooth cadence of our steps lifted my spirit. Back and forth, our bodies moved in perfect unison. With his cheek pressed to mine, my partner's refined dance moves carried me to a higher plane. I felt an engaging intimacy void of sexual suggestion. My confidence soared as we swayed to a cha-cha tune.

With each twirl and turn, my eyes avoided the bar, fearful that a scowl from Bob would melt the magic of the moment. I was in paradise. When a faster number began to play, however, my partner and I agreed to sit this one out.

Oh, how I wished I could have stayed and danced all evening! But with Bob sitting nearby, I decided to leave while things were still pleasant. I hugged my mother-in-law, said goodbye to Bob, and nodded to my dance partner. His wink and reassuring smile boosted my self-assurance as I glided from the room.

"Yes, yes, yes!" I whispered, pumping my arm as I waited for my car. "I am not a reject. Someone thinks I'm attractive."

Silently, I spoke to my Father God. *That was an angel, wasn't it? You arranged a celestial intervention. You sent an angel to dance with me and raise my spirits. God, are You trying to show me that Your justice is far more pleasing than my pathetic plans for revenge?*

I had wanted to get even with Bob. But why? Petty paybacks

would not bring restitution.

And about that facelift? How could a wrinkle-free face heal my deep self-image scars? What I needed was an internal adjustment. I humbly began to take a personal searching and fearless inventory.

Through it all, I have been reassured of God's love for me. No facial surgery or name change would disavow His commitment to my well-being. I am His and He is mine.

I had looked for validation from others, but an angel—a Bright Morning Star—led me with His affirming love. He taught me to know when to "sit this one out" and when to walk away from volatile situations. Simply put, it would be up to me to recognize and respect my discomfort zone. Each time I accomplish that, I add value to myself.

Encounters with angels are fleeting, but they deliver meaningful messages. Brief but powerful, my divine meeting produced a long overdue reunion with self-respect. My angelic dance partner taught me how to change my dysfunctional two-step marathon into an eternal dance of dignity and grace.

> *Then the woman went to her husband and told him, "A man of God came to me. He looked like an angel of God, very awesome. I didn't ask him where he came from, and he didn't tell me his name"* (Judges 13:6 NIV).

Notes:

27. Senior Citizen Dating: A New Kind of Courage

The Journey

More than two decades since the divorce and I was still single. In all that time, I'd gone out with only three men. What was wrong with me?

When it came to meeting men, I was a pushover for the silent type. I believed I was the one who would help them come out of their shell. So at first, that was the kind of man I was interested in dating.

Henry was my first suitor soon after my husband and I separated. His calming manner and my outgoing nature convinced me we'd be a perfect fit. His magnetic smile and twinkling eyes reeled me in. We went to dinner and to Broadway shows at the Bucks County Playhouse in New Hope. We enjoyed quiet summer evenings on the patio I once shared with my husband. Only this time, Henry and I were discussing how to manage our pending divorces.

On one such night, I sensed Henry wanted more than just a goodnight kiss. In that instant, I convinced myself we were not such an ideal match after all. His desire for intimacy was my cue to say goodbye.

At the time, my dream was to move to Florida. After decades of cultivating a dysfunctional marriage, I would not let a serious affair derail my plans. That was the end of the relationship with Henry.

The Healing

My dream had come true. I was in paradise. Seagulls swooped in front of me as I walked barefoot along Lake Worth beach, returning the cheerful smiles of my fellow Floridians. Since I walked the same route daily, I recognized people who did the same. Including a tall man with graying hair who nodded whenever we passed each other. Sometimes I spotted him at band concerts in the park.

One night at a library fund-raising event, the man came up to me. "Hi, I've seen you at the beach and around town. I noticed you're always alone. My name is Jake. Mind if I sit next to you?"

He seemed so self-assured.

I shifted in my seat. "Please, sit down." I had to remind myself to lighten up. *Relax, Diane, it's a library. He's not picking you up at a singles bar.*

Casual and buoyant, Jake managed the conversation. His last job as a professor at Penn State explained his expert communication skills. He was also a musician who liked steel drum music.

It was fate, destiny, karma all rolled into one happy surprise. I was from Pennsylvania, and I loved steel drum music!

Before the evening was over, I had accepted my first Friday night date in years.

That first night, we sat at the oceanfront restaurant listening to spirited Caribbean tunes. The melodic waves reaching out to hug the shore lifted me up, and the calypso melodies transported me to an island where carefree pleasures reigned. The music and evening ended at my front door with a soft kiss.

When Jake called for a second date, I said no. I'm not sure why. Jake had a lot going for him. He was respectful and intelligent and, most notably, on our date he'd only had one glass of wine. Could it have been the fear of intimacy that prompted me to turn him down?

Whatever the reason, I had decided to continue my journey— alone.

But was I really alone?

GOD said, "My presence will go with you. I'll see the journey to the end" (Exodus 33:14 MSG).

28. Being Alone Doesn't Mean Being Lonely

The Journey

Her blonde hair hidden under a straw hat, the woman clicked the car fob to lock her Honda. As she walked down the sidewalk, she tried to appear casual. Her straw clutch purse tightly by her side, she looked around. First left, then right, peering over her sunglasses for a lone man nursing a latte.

No, this was not amateur detective Jessica Fletcher scanning a trendy outdoor café in an episode of *Murder She Wrote*. That was me, on my first blind date. And boy, was it awkward.

After my neighbor told me about a friend whose wife had succumbed to cancer, she'd insisted, "You and Mel would be perfect together."

Against my better judgment, I'd agreed to meet him for coffee.

The retired New York executive and I met at a local coffee bar. Mel was nice, but it didn't take long for me to realize this sad person, who looked a little too much like my ex-father-in-law, was emotionally bleeding to death. Before I had a chance to pick up my steaming mug of decaf coffee, my date pulled out his cell phone and showed me pictures of his deceased wife.

"She's lovely," I told him. Immediately, my codependent tendencies wanted to soothe the sorrow only he could work through. From my well-practiced enabler playbook, I opened with a question I knew would change his downcast mood. "Tell me about your kids and grandkids. Do they live in Florida or New York?"

A slight smile appeared as he refocused on what he had instead of what he'd lost. From pride in his family to overcoming a painful knee replacement surgery, Mel dominated the rest of the conversation.

"I'm still active," he bragged with a wink. "After physical therapy, I got right back into swimming fifty laps a day." My new friend sat back in the brightly painted bistro chair. "My job in the city was challenging, but the weekends with my family made it all worthwhile."

Then, as if a seasonal storm cloud had drifted over without warning, he began to scroll through his phone again. When he found the picture he was looking for, he handed me the phone. "Here's my wife Joann and me on our last cruise."

I placed my hand on his and in my sympathetic counseling voice said, "Mel, I think you need more time to heal. In the meantime, I'll be praying you meet the right someone for you."

With sad, puppy dog eyes, he looked at me and confessed, "I thought I did. You."

Gulp! After one hour, two cups of black coffee, and half a bagel, he thought we were on our way to being a couple. The only thing he knew about me was whatever our mutual friend had told him. Mel did not ask about my family, my lifestyle, or my future goals.

Absorbed in my own grief, it never occurred to me that widowers and men going through a divorce also hurt. Frank, Henry, and Mel were all seeking a quick replacement for their wives. These men were not looking for permanent solutions. They wanted immediate gratification. They wanted someone to make them feel better—to take away their pain.

They were looking for an enabler.

The fact that I didn't fall for their needy but honest lines meant I must be getting better. I no longer felt guilty enough to stay with a melancholic man and try to fix him.

Yes, I seemed to be getting better.

Or was I?

The Healing

More recently, I came across the term *counter-codependent*. I had thought I knew all there was to know about the dynamics of codependency. As I studied the characteristics of a counter-codependent, I decided to re-examine my co-addictive behaviors. Again.

When I did, I experienced a revelation. Along with being a fixer, I also wore a hard hat with *avoidance* stenciled across it. It seems I had gone from being a busybody to an isolationist.

In the old days, I'd loved getting involved with and helping others. I would put myself last in order to assist everyone else. Helping to the point of playing the martyr was a role that could easily land me the Best Actress in a Drama Series Award. Now I wondered if early abandonment issues were causing me to shy away from commitment. Why else would the opinionated woman living inside me keep retreating from involvement?

My search for answers taught me to keep healthy boundaries, grow in confidence, then go spread the word. Nowhere did it mention seclusion as a stepping-stone to growth.

That past holiday season, I challenged my shelter-in-place mindset and accepted several party invitations. One pleasant evening found me enjoying dinner with friends and their family. At a neighbor's open house, Christmas and popular tunes from the 60's filled the night air. Still, my classic conditioning dictated I be the first one to leave the party—any party. The gracious hostess wrapped her arm around my shoulder and as she escorted me to the door, she commented. "Diane, you certainly know how to mingle. You didn't know the other guests, and I worried that I would have to entertain you. Not so. Every time I looked, you were engaged in animated conversation."

It was a fun evening and Lara's compliment reinforced I no longer had to act like a victim. I don't want to be a victim. I don't have to be a victim. My healthy spirit has removed the quarantine sign. I am a new creation.

Now we look inside, and what we see is that anyone united with the Messiah gets a fresh start, is created new. The old life is gone; a new life burgeons [flourishes]! (2 Corinthians 5:17 MSG).

Part Twelve: A Lily Blooms One Day at a Time

29. A Patient Plants a Seed

The Journey

Daily dosages of warm sunshine, white sand beaches, and vibrant flowers. Who wouldn't feel better after basking by day in balmy breezes and spending nights in dreamy tropical settings? The benefits of Florida living offset the stress I felt during the hours at work. I had two jobs, one for the school district and one at a drug and alcohol recovery center. Overall things were good and, I believed, life could not have been kinder.

Until I regressed, that is. I took on problems not of my making and defended them as if they were my own. Unhealthy concerns for others was like a throbbing scab that kept popping open when I least expected. This time, a relentless pain in my abdomen resulted in a trip to the local hospital.

"Nurse, no. Stop! Please don't do that."

Like chalk scratching across a blackboard, the metal hooks screeched along the narrow track. A shiver went through me as I begged the angel in green scrubs not to open the curtain that separated the two hospital beds.

"Please, don't push the curtain back any farther."

"All right, Diane," she promised. "Just give me a minute to hook up her IV. Then I'll reposition the bed and close the curtain."

My request sounded harsh, even to me, but the truth was I couldn't bear to see the elderly woman in the other bed. Seeing her brought on waves of nausea. Blood-soaked gauze covered her frail-looking arm and droplets of red splattered across the front of her hospital gown. We had to share the semi-private room, but I didn't have to look at her physical distress.

The nurse closed the curtain, but that didn't block out the sound of the patient's lament. Over and over, she begged, "Please take me home. I want to go home."

A woman's voice tried to shush her. "You can't go home, Mom. You need to be here so the doctors and nurses can give you the around-the-clock care you need."

I lay there trying to relax. It was impossible.

Then the woman called out to me. "Excuse me," she said. "I heard the nurse call you Diane. My name is Diane, too. Well, actually, it's Diana. My mother, Lily, is your roommate."

"Hi, Diana," I began in a weak, apologetic attempt at conversation. "I couldn't help but overhear you tell the aide how you and your mother had waited all night in the emergency room until a bed became available. You must be exhausted."

"Oh, you have no idea. I haven't had an uninterrupted night's sleep in weeks. I can't wait to go home and get a good night's rest."

Before the next drip from the IV hit my veins, resentment trickled into my brain. I envisioned what my night would look like. Diana would get her wish. She'd sleep peacefully, but her mother would keep me awake all night!

The Healing

Such insensitive thoughts confused me. If this mother and daughter had known what I was thinking, they would not have identified me as a Christian. Like the disciple, Peter, I had forgotten my faith and compassion came from the Lord. Now, my thoughts denied I ever knew the Man whose example I professed to follow.

No one commanded me to take over. Nobody said, "Diane, regardless of your condition, you have to stay awake and play night nurse to Lily." It was my own convoluted sense of responsibility that goaded me into believing I was responsible for Lily's care. As a life-long codependent, I fed an insatiable need to try to rescue everyone I met. I practiced compulsive caregiving, and then complained about all I did for others. When I failed to step in and help, guilt ate away at me. No wonder my hospital stay was due to gastrointestinal bleeding—most likely caused by a stomach ulcer.

Isolated on my side of the hospital room, gave me time to beat myself up about my unsympathetic attitude. Right on cue, guilt showed up and turned on the blame that triggered the stomach acids and added to my abdominal pain. I lay there in agony.

The cycle had to stop. With my head on my pillow, I began to meditate on the one true Comforter, Jesus. In this quiet time, I came to understand He had never asked me to assume His role. No one had asked me to pull out my IV and become Lily's room martyr. Heck, with my out-of-control victim mentality, I could be the floor martyr. The hospital martyr, even.

No, this would no longer be my role. All my Creator expected of me was to be His ambassador of kindness and love. My Higher Power's request was simple—let Diane be Diane and let God be God.

What I learned from this experience was the need to set healthy boundaries. No hospital curtain or self-imposed seclusion could separate me from His compassionate care. There is no barricade limiting God's love.

And I am convinced that nothing can ever separate us from God's love. Neither death nor life, neither angels nor demons, neither our fears for today nor our worries about tomorrow—not even the powers of hell can separate us from God's love (Romans 8:38).

Notes:

30. The Gardener Nurtures the Seed

The Journey

After Diana left, the moaning on the other side of the curtain stopped. I prayed sleep would tiptoe in.

Constant dings and the loud swish of elevator doors opening and closing drifted into the room. I overheard change-of-shift personnel whispering, patients calling out for nurses. Sleep did not arrive. I didn't want my bed buddy Mr. Worry to hop in and make himself comfortable, so I turned over and prayed. *God, I am just as tired as Lily's daughter Diana. Please, please let my roommate sleep until morning. I need to get some rest, too.*

The late-night anxiety I felt in this cold, unfamiliar place was no different from what I had experienced on countless other occasions. So many fretful nights I had tossed and turned, waiting for the signal to relax. When the car headlights cut across the shadowy bedroom ceiling, I would let out a sigh of relief. After yet another night of drinking, my spouse had pulled into the driveway. Finally, the sign I could sleep. Or pretend I was asleep.

A gurgled cry ended my reflection.

"Diana, where are you when I need you?" Lily cried from under an oxygen mask.

A light from the hall stole across the darkened hospital wall. My stomach churned as I gazed at the curtain. I predicted this would happen. This is the beginning of a long, sleepless night.

Lily's mumbling curbed any effort I made to get to dreamland. She rambled on with unfinished thoughts. When her jumbled dialogue stopped, I saw shadows moving across the curtain. Any flirtation with sleep ended.

A male nurse came in the small room. "Oh no, Ms. Lily, you pulled out your IV. There's blood all over."

Yuck, did he have to be so graphic?

He spoke softly to her as he cleaned her up, providing kind words of comfort. Then he left.

Quiet returned, and I began to doze.

"Help me, help me. I'm stuck," cried the little woman on the other side of the partition.

The Healing

Jolted from a much too short siesta, I had an idea. Rather than fight the endless night's interruptions, I would become the surrogate daughter.

I called to Lily, "Please, don't move. Don't hurt yourself. I'm right beside you. I'll ring for the nurse." At the same time, I prayed, *Please, God, if it will calm her, let her think I'm her Diana.*

I reached as far as my IV would allow so I could move the curtain back. I wanted to see if my roommate was stuck between the bars of the bed.

"It's okay," I consoled. "I'm right beside you. The nurse is coming. I promise I won't leave you."

Not only had this fragile woman roused me from sleep, she had aroused my compassion as well. I reached through the bars of her bed to rub her scrawny hand. "Lie still, Honey I'm here with you. You're going to be okay."

But would *I* be okay?

An expression of confusion and fear stared back at me. She looked lost. The more I comforted her, the more I found I wanted to protect this delicate wilting flower from further trauma. My old self, the real Diane, the one who truly cared for others, was reemerging.

In a small hospital room, God had brought two ailing women together. There He taught the younger of the two that genuine caring requires one critical component—His presence. When I pushed aside the shroud of indifference, I discovered our Creator had never left Lily—or me. He had been present throughout the night. He resurrected my spirit, and I gave myself permission to forgive my lack of empathy.

The God of Light helped me push away denial's veil of self-abasing lies. Is it any wonder I want to walk step-in-step with Him?

> *At that moment the curtain in the sanctuary of the Temple was torn in two, from top to bottom. The earth shook, rocks split apart, and tombs opened. The bodies of many godly men and women who had died were raised from the dead* (Matthew 27:51-52).

Notes.

31. Seeds of Love Burst through the Veil

The Journey

When the nurse returned, he repositioned Lily in the bed and called for an aide. While the two angels of mercy tended to her, I overheard one say the doctor had given new orders. They would be moving her to the intensive care unit in the morning.

As the gossamer blush of the rising sun warmed our room, I leaned over to check on the women in the bed next to me. She appeared to be asleep.

After the nurse removed my IV, I walked to the bathroom. Now that I was free to move, I realized my insensitivity had restrained me more than the intravenous apparatus in my arm. God's grace was repositioning me from being wedged in callous thoughts and actions.

As I passed by Lily's bed, I saw her eyes following me. I returned her look with a slight smile and wondered, *Lily, are you looking for comfort in a stranger's smile? Or searching for the familiarity of your daughter's touch?*

The Healing

The newness of the morning light helped me look past the life-saving tubes and monitors that overshadowed Lily's slight frame and straight into her dark eyes. In her eyes, I saw understanding. Mesmerized, I searched further and found forgiveness. Unable to move, her gaze filled me with calm assurance—it was as though I was looking into the eyes of Christ.

I couldn't utter a sound. Lily didn't speak with her mouth, but her eyes spoke His message of love. Face-to-face, God looked deep into my soul and made me whole.

In my effort to keep a curtained barrier between Lily and myself,

I had almost lost the chance to look into the eyes of God.

Nothing could veil my tears as I stood motionless at the foot of her bed. I took courage by the hand and with the other reached out to touch Lily. I whispered, "Everything will be all right," and gently patted her pale legs with their bulging varicose veins. "You'll be well cared for in the intensive care unit."

From under the plastic oxygen mask came a muffled, "Thank you, Diane."

She knew my name. She knew I was not her Diana. How could she suddenly be so coherent?

I prompted her, checking to see if she really knew it was me and not her daughter. "You are very brave. You did well last night. Now you'll have specially trained staff at your side. You'll never be alone."

Without blinking, Lily's deep-set eyes stared me down. "Thank you, Diane."

She knew.

Throughout the long night, I had role-played at being her daughter, when all along she knew it was me who comforted her. Lily knew the difference.

A dream-like tranquility settled in my heart. With a smile on my face and in my heart, I smoothed the hospital gown around her legs and said a silent prayer for her.

Compassion had helped me look into the piercing eyes of God and, when I did, I found my true self. There was no lingering guilt. He is real, and He raised me up—to love again.

Whenever, though, they turn to face God ...God removes the veil and there they are—face-to-face! They suddenly recognize that God is a living, personal presence, not a piece of chiseled stone... (2 Corinthians 3:16-17 MSG).

Part Thirteen: Healing the Hole in Our Heart

32. Recovering from the Inside Out

The Journey

"No, Dr. Cavanaugh, no. There's no way I can clean and dress Sandy's wound. You'll have to stitch up that gaping hole in her chest. Now!"

This was so typical of me, telling the veterinarian how to do his job. And me without a medical license. Still, he had to know I couldn't do what he wanted me to do. I couldn't bear to look at the pus and blood oozing out of our golden retriever's gaping chest wound, let alone touch it.

Staring at the well-respected small town doctor, I continued to make my case. "Warm compresses and ointment will never work. Don't you see how deep the lesion is? She has nine puppies to feed. I'll never be able to keep her underside clean and her pups happy."

Sandy lay motionless on the stainless steel slab. Her pleading eyes were locked in a helpless gaze with my son Rob. The vet continued to clean her abscess.

This was my first experience with a dog and her litter. In one short week, I had learned so much. Sandy's devotion to her nine newborns could have been a segment on the *DogTV* channel. She knew exactly what to do for her babies. She fed them, licked them clean, and nudged them when it was time to give another pup a turn at a nipple. Strong animal instincts were in place. This new mother had it under control. I didn't have to do a thing. A refreshing reprieve for a codependent like myself.

Until the morning I went to put a clean beach towel on the overcrowded doggie bed. When Sandy slowly rolled over, I jumped back in horror. In between the puppies tugging at her teats was a large, cavernous hole. Right in the middle of her chest. An unrehearsed scream flooded my throat as I turned and gagged.

My queasiness would have to wait. I bucked up, then knelt down to get a closer look. An open canal in her chest area exposed layers of raw flesh. Like a squishy hollowed-out tomato, each fold deepened to a bloodier shade of red. Dangling tissue oozed out of the inflamed wound.

How could I have missed seeing this earlier? I blamed myself for not taking proper care of our furry family member.

At the vet's office, I begged Dr. Cavanaugh to fix her ASAP. Instead, the sage old doctor looked over his glasses at me, raising his thick gray eyebrows. This was his way of saying he would ignore my suggestions. He continued to work on the exhausted young mother in his care.

When he was done, he turned to me. "Mrs. Jellen, Sandy's abscessed mastitis has to heal from the inside out. I won't pretend it's going to be easy. Truth is, this will be a slow, painstaking process. Getting Sandy well is going to require a good deal of attention on your part. You'll have to clean the pus from the lesion and apply ointment to the infected area several times a day. This is the only way she will heal completely."

Before we left his office, the vet had one more warning. "Don't be surprised if you have to wean the pups. That means you'll have to bottle-feed all nine of them."

Armed with a jar of ointment, a roll of gauze, and a strong dose of determination, I followed Rob as he carried our big brave girl out of the veterinarian's office.

The Healing

Sandy's story is one I often share when people ask me how I maintained my sanity and kept my family together after my ex-husband lost his battle with alcohol abuse. When people ask me how long it took to let go and move on, I tell them about Sandy.

Our patient golden retriever refused to give up. Despite her pain,

Sandy did not attempt to solicit sympathy as she struggled to keep her family fed. She never complained about how many times she had to get up during the night. Without whimpering, our lovable canine did what she had to do. She followed her natural instinct to nurture.

As soon as we got home from the veterinarian's office, Rob laid our beloved pet on her bed. The whimpering puppies huddling together in the opposite corner caught their mother's scent. Dozens of tiny paws scrambled as the pups attached themselves to her. A warm, wet nose guided them into place and she began to feed her hungry litter.

When all the pups were finished feeding, Sandy rolled away and rested her head. She'd had a rough day. Now it was my turn to take care of her needs. I pulled on a pair of rubber gloves. As instructed, I reached into the wide-lipped jar, covered the yellow gloves with salve, and gently slathered the outside of the wound, working inward.

This regimen continued. Within a few days, the angry red skin had calmed. As I repeated the steps prescribed by Dr. Cavanaugh, the hole began to shrink. The deep laceration *was* healing from the inside out. A soft gray color replaced the fire engine red as the gap continued to close. Sandy was on the mend.

Her recovery would never have been possible without the day-to-day, step-by-step application. It was indeed a slow, painstaking process, but one that led to a complete healing. All the while, this determined mother managed to satisfy her puppies' needs. I never had to bottle feed them.

The day did come, however, when Sandy began to distance herself from the demanding puppies at her side. Their tiny teeth were coming in, making it uncomfortable for her to nurse. This was her sign to let go. She knew enabling her pups by allowing them to take more from her would not benefit her offspring. Each time they tried to latch on, she'd detach them from her teats. It was time for them to adjust and mature on their own.

Sometimes enablers confuse detachment with abandonment. It took a wise golden retriever to teach me that detaching with love was, in fact, a silent strength.

Dr. Cavanaugh was correct about Sandy's recovery. I doubt he knew his veterinarian training and wise counsel applied to my healing as well. Detaching from obsessive enabling has been an excruciatingly slow process. But it *is* healing. My awareness of the disease of addiction and co-addiction has helped me to discover the perfect soothing balm. In my Higher Power, I have found the one who could close the hole in my spirit before it became too big to suture. By working on my open wound and moving inward to my spiritual core, He healed me from the inside out.

My understanding of detachment from co-addictive behaviors became clearer because of the unconditional love of a furry canine. When I remember Sandy, I see the wind blow through her flaxen coat as she runs through sun-drenched fields. A confident, carefree leader of the pack who knew when to trust her gut and when to let go.

Sandy lived many of the Al-Anon slogans I try to practice. Each time I dressed her wounds, she made it clear that *easy does it* beats rushing to a temporary quick fix. With nine mouths to feed, this mother monitored her pups, teaching them *first things first*. Our entire family supported her through her healing and, with a thankful tilt of her head, she assured us *this too shall pass*. Her example showed me the commitment behind the emotionally challenging mantra *detach with love*. Thanks to Sandy, I began to *trust my gut. One day at a time* I am learning to *let go and let God.*

> *"I will give you back your health and heal your wounds,"* says the LORD... (Jeremiah 30:14-17 NLT).

144

33. Trade of a Lifetime

The Journey

The warm December sun danced across the small lake outside my patio. *Do it, Diane,* I told myself as I dialed the number. After four rings, however, my call went to voicemail. As I left a message for my brother, I wondered if Joe would return my call like his message promised. Or would the missed call signal another split in our recently renewed relationship?

Joe was hot or cold, up or down, always unpredictable. As I basked in the sunshine and waited for his return call, I thought of the years we never shared as siblings, the period in our lives when my brother took a twenty-year hiatus from communicating with his mother, sisters, aunts, and uncles. During that time, he had married and divorced twice, overcome his addiction to alcohol and nicotine, fathered four children, and help raise three grandkids.

A week passed before I reached out and called again. After the third ring, I heard my brother's long raspy, "Hellooo."

Joe was in an up mood so the conversation was cordial. Then he posed a surprising question. "Diane, would you do me a favor?"

"Sure," I answered.

"Last summer you told me you made arrangements to donate your body to research after you pass away. Where can I get information about that? I want to do the same thing."

"Since your doctors are affiliated with Hershey Medical Center, you could ask them how to get the forms you'll need. I'm sure they can help you get started."

After thanking me, he asked how hot it was in Florida. While he whistled and whined about the cold weather up north, my mind traveled to another season of our lives when we competed in a simpler childhood exchange.

It was a hot summer day, and Joe and I were in the middle of a heated trading card negotiation.

"Joe, I'll trade ya 'Stan The Man' Musial for Duke Snider."

"Nope."

"Please, please. The next time you have to go down the cellar to get a bucket of coal for the kitchen stove, I'll do it for you. Okay, okay? Do we have a deal?"

I was only seven when I bargained with my eight-year-old brother for what I believed to be the best baseball card deal I'd ever make. Growing up in an extended family that included four uncles and a loving grandfather, sports was the main topic in the family butcher shop. Sports talk spilled into the adjoining kitchen of our large homestead. In the early 1950s, there were only three television channels. ABC, CBS, and NBC filled us with wonder. On summer weekends, however, our television was permanently set to one station—baseball. Consequently, I knew most of the teams and the players. And I had a crush on the handsome, full-cheeked, tobacco-chewing Brooklyn Dodgers centerfielder Duke Snider.

The day we talked body donations, Joe and I were trading something more meaningful than the official Topps™ baseball cards. Now we were swapping information on how to recycle our earthly bodies in the hope that others could benefit.

This wasn't Joe's only tradeoff. Before he quit smoking and overcame his dependence on alcohol, Joe had traded his diseased larynx for an artificial voice box. My defiant brother also swapped his relationship with his mother, sister Peg, and me in order to form a stronger bond with substance abuse. Twenty years later, he stopped drinking and allowed us back into his life.

Curious, I switched the phone to my other hand. "Joe, why are you asking about donating your body now? Are you okay?"

Between the cell phone delay and the garbled words from his

manmade larynx, I strained to hear his answer.

"Had another MRI and there's an inoperable mass on my left lung. I've started radiation and chemotherapy treatments. The doctors say I have six months, maybe a year." He paused, then added, "But the really good news is I've been approved for a thirty-year mortgage."

Despite his physical ailments, my sixty-nine-year-old brother had retained his sense of humor. Now it was my turn to exchange pointless social media searches for meaningful investigation. I promised to get the required forms from the humanity gift website and mail them to him.

We had come a long way from trading baseball cards.

The Healing

Joe never filled out the forms. He lived alone, and when the mail began piling up on his porch, the local police investigated. When they entered his home, they found cancer had played the final card. My sibling had traded in this life for the promise of a resurrected one with his Heavenly Father.

Joe did not have time to sign off on his good intentions. Hidden between his unopened mail and the local grocery store flyers was a large manila envelope containing the body donation forms.

He didn't live long enough to attend another family reunion. He never applied for that long-term mortgage, either.

Over the course of our lifetimes, we are free to make choices, some honorable, others we may later regret. What I grieve most are the years Joe and I were not in touch, the years he traded his family for an obstinate heart. At the time, however, there was not a single concession I could have offered him that would've made him change his mind.

I don't remember if my brother ever gave me that Duke Snider baseball card, but I am grateful he gave me the last years of his life. The end-of-days my sister and I shared with our prodigal brother taught me the one thing we cannot barter for is the length of our lives. I am thankful we kissed and made up before it was too late.

In the end, alcohol abuse, smoking, and cancer ravaged Joe's body. But self-blame and shame could not destroy the love we shared.

> *"Then I will make up to you for the years that the swarming locust has eaten ..."* (Joel 2:25 NASB).

34. Bruised Spirits: A Slow-Healing Process

The Journey

I see trees of green, red roses too. I see them bloom, for me and you.
And I think to myself, what a wonderful world.

Forearm stretch. Check. Hamstring stretch. Check. Ankle flex. Check. What better way to end a water aerobics class then stretching to Louis Armstrong's classic rendition of *What a Wonderful World.*

"Well, that's it for me." I was always the first to leave. "See you tomorrow," I shouted as I did water lunges to the edge of the pool.

Behind me, a friend's voice halted my steps. "Oh yeah, that's right. It's 9:00 AM. You better keep to your tight schedule. You're always in such a hurry, Diane. What would it hurt if you stayed a little longer?"

I turned to face Roxie, but no words came out of my mouth. The old Diane would have been ready with a volley of stinging answers. *Why the ?&?$%# do you care?* My expertise, developed over a long history of launching verbal abuse, would have put her under with a simple sentence. *It's none of your blankety-blank business what kind of schedule I keep.*

Waist deep in the heated pool, however, I remained speechless as Roxie continued her critique from the deep end, her flowered bathing cap pushed up and strands of her henna dyed hair peeked through. "Diane, you're so serious. Even the books you read have a sober message. Did you ever think of relaxing with a cozy murder mystery? I read cookbook murder novels," she added. As if her taste in "literature" should satisfy me too.

I waited, hoping she was done. But she wasn't finished yet.

Still treading water, she said, "You never go to the lighthearted flicks. The films you pick all have to do with depressing history like the Holocaust, or some heavy-themed documentary. When I go to the movies I like to come out feeling entertained, not depressed."

When I reclaimed my voice, I took on an apologetic tone. "Maybe you're right. However, I'm trying different genres to explore new perspectives. I like books and movies that enlighten as well as entertain."

My explanation wasn't sufficient for my swimming pool buddy. Her putdowns kept coming after she made her way to my side. "I'm not sure you realize it, Diane, but when we're talking, you're still doing your exercise routine. Girl, you better learn to relax."

I stopped marching in place. "Roxie, I have a timetable. I like to be home, showered, and writing by 10 AM."

Turning away, I took defiant lunges that propelled me to the ladder instead of dunking her under the water like I wanted to. I pulled on my beach cover-up and grabbed my water weights, leaving her behind.

Like pesky ants at a picnic, Roxie's comments continued to invade my thoughts. Years of building a positive self-image had been eaten away in one blistery conversation. One minute I was scolding myself about how right she was about me, that I was too regimented. The next moment I would sort out her judgmental rant by trying to justify my productive lifestyle. I was in a freefall relapse.

The internal conflict began to wear me down. There was only one thing to do: retrace my steps. When I got to the 4th Step and *made a searching and fearless inventory*, I began to feel better. I was reclaiming control. One of my strong points was effective planning skills, and I would not apologize for that.

In order to avoid future confrontations, I adopted a bright new morning schedule and arrived at the pool before the exercise class started. When I left the pool each day, Roxie was just arriving. She would ask, "Leaving the pool already?"

Every day I had a different reason. "The handyman is coming

today." Or, "I have to walk my friend's dog."

After years of 12 Step meetings, I was still swimming around the elephant in the pool. It had to stop. I needed to find a way to rid myself of the mammoth in my head.

Days passed before I picked up the phone and called my friend. "Roxie, I haven't been honest with you. The past several times we ran into each other, you asked why I went to the pool so early. Instead of being truthful, I made up excuses. I'm calling to tell you the real reason I changed my exercise schedule."

"Oh?" The cell phone delay did not disguise the inflection in her voice. She was waiting for an explanation.

I shook my head in disbelief. At my age, I shouldn't have to describe my bruised spirit to a friend. We should be beyond middle-school behavior, right? Sad to say, we weren't.

"The reason I stopped going to the water exercise class with you is the same reason I avoid the women's club luncheons and bus trips. I don't want to get involved in petty gossip. I had hoped limiting my involvement would shield me from this kind of thing. The morning you recited everything you didn't like about my lifestyle blew my avoidance plans out of the water."

"I'm sorry *if* I hurt your feelings," Roxie insisted. "I didn't mean to. I hope this doesn't mean you're going to stop coming to the pool."

"No, I'm not going to stop. That's why I called. To let you know why I decided to go earlier."

She apologized, again stating, "...*if I* hurt your feelings."

It wasn't a matter of *if* she'd hurt my feelings. She had. What troubled me was why I had allowed someone to take me to the woodshed and emotionally beat the worth out of *my* self.

Again.

The Healing

It wasn't complicated. Something as simple as adjusting my swim time was what *detach with love* looks like. I was learning the fine art of focusing on improving myself, not others.

When I recall my interactions with Roxie, I see my steady footsteps moving forward. I'm not angry with my friend. The truth is, in her, I saw the person I used to be. The enabler who grew up believing she had to fix everyone. Because of Roxie, I'm more aware of my efforts to manipulate others. Back then, I called it "helping." After years of playing the role of a controlling extrovert, I now recognize the difference between outgoing and obnoxious.

On the morning Roxie recited everything she thought I did wrong, I remained calm. I didn't realize it at the time, but I was processing the situation before reacting. My silence did not mean weakness. It revealed a recovering codependent who was comfortable in her own skin. I had become a more reflective person, one who didn't go on an insulting rant I would regret later. Contentment requires surrender, and when I gave up my defensive nature, I walked away with a peaceful spirit.

It may sound like I have it all together, but I'm not fooling myself. I know recovery is an ongoing process. Evidence that I had slipped was revealed when I found myself taking my friend's inventory by questioning her motives and insecurities. I had to remind myself how her issues were not my issues. What I learned was the only way to lead the elephant out of the room (or the pool) is one-step, one day at a time.

Because of Roxie, I have a greater appreciation of myself. I am okay with me just the way I am. Now all I have to do is remember this the next time I'm under attack for the way I am choosing to live.

Now, where was I? Oh, yeah. *I see trees of green, red roses too, and I think to myself, what a wonderful world.*

What a wildly wonderful world, GOD! You made it all, with wisdom at your side, made earth overflow with your wonderful creations (Psalm 104:24 MSG).

Notes:

Part Fourteen: The Potter's Touch

35. Removing Character Defects: The Potter Remolds a Codependent's Heart

Shattered.
Dreams in pieces.
After thirty years,
Separation, divorce.
A rudderless codependent.
No one to enable.
No one to control.
An empty urn.
A crushed vessel.
Life without a purpose.

I need a new direction.
Twelve Step meetings.
Support Groups.
Would college mend my broken shards?
An Old Testament course to calm my harried soul.
Not to learn religious practices
but practical living.

First night of class, dimmed lights, soft music
a small lump of clay on each desk.
Professor's instructions,
"Relax, breathe, form your clay.
Listen to what your spirit says."

She reads Jeremiah 18:1-4.

The LORD gave another message to Jeremiah.
He said, "Go down to the potter's shop,
and I will speak to you there."

So I did as he told me and found the potter working at his
wheel.
But the jar he was making did not turn out as he had hoped,
so he crushed it into a lump of clay again and started over.

Silence falls.
No voices, no classroom chatter.
The stillness feels foreign.
Where's my daily dose of drama?
I miss frenzied.

My spirit settles.
Eyes closed, imagination called into play.
I squeeze a simple piece of clay.
My forceful grip forms a ball.

A small voice calls out
Stop, you're going too fast.
Slow down.
Take time,
experience the motion.
Touch, feel the harmony.
There—that's better.

A relationship
between two forces begins.
Hands and clay, working in unison
like legs and pedals on a bike
heading somewhere,
but where?

Kneading offers comfort
an intimate closeness.

A container, a vessel
begins to form.
Oh, no! Cracks along the edges.
Add water, I tell myself
water soothes dry, open wounds.

I press on.
Too much
too thin
too yielding
too accommodating.
Must have a stronger base,
must hold worth.

Redo, I discern my spirit say.
I don't have time, I wrestle.

"There is time left,
My time," says the Potter.
"Form a stronger foundation.
If the base is solid
it will hold
it will take in—give out
it will have a purpose,
My purpose," reminds my Lord.

Amazed, I find
there *is* still time.

My new form *is* stronger.
I can serve His purpose.
I will retain worth
His Worth,

drawn from the well of Living Water!

But wait.
The flaws, the uneven fractures.
I know, I'll smooth them over.

"Let them go," exclaims my Lord, the Potter.
"Scallops signify diversity
the ability to balance your life
to work, to play, to laugh again."

I muse, *scallops*
what a pretty word.

Where I see cracks, imperfection
the Lord sees beauty.

He continues, "The Crevices
my protection
my hiding place for your safety
my perfect dwelling for your retreat.
Embrace the brokenness of life to learn and grow."

The Potter directs,
"It is finished for now.
Let it be."

Still, I stroke the rough clay pot
like a mother putting the finishing touch
on her child's silky hair.
Not because anything is out of place,
but solely to touch as He does
lovingly.
To caress and be caressed

by my Maker, the Potter.

To be His vessel
until my earthly time is no more.

Notes:

Acknowledgements

With the 12 Steps as a roadmap, I have navigated through countless day-to-day challenges and encountered many roadblocks. At each milepost, my children and grandkids, family, friends, sponsors, and strangers have powered my progress. It has been affirming to learn my future is not about me fixing others, it's about letting go and letting God.

The way forward has been possible because of the men and women I've met in "the rooms." Adding to my positive outlook are my friends at *Within Recovery Café and Bookstore* in Lake Worth, Florida.

My appreciation extends to my fellow authors at the Monday morning writer's group: Jennifer Broderick, Judith Brooker, Jason Bonderoff, and Michael Cantwell. Once again, my editor son Jonathan, grandson Ian O'Connell, and my friend, author and editor Virginia Aronson infused their expertise and along with ThatFormattingLady.com helped shape *Heaven Heals a Codependent's Heart* into a finished product I am proud to share with others.

To those not mentioned because of promises of anonymity, my respect and prayers are with you as you continue your healing journey. For my new friends venturing out of the zone of denial for the first time, I pray you give yourself permission to trust your Higher Power. He is in the business of healing bruised hearts. Together, we will continue the steps to recovery and hope eternal.

Beginning with the First Step—Where it all began

THE TWELVE STEPS OF ALCOHOLICS ANONYMOUS

1. We admitted we were powerless over alcohol—that our lives had become unmanageable.

2. Came to believe that a Power greater than ourselves could restore us to sanity.

3. Made a decision to turn our will and our lives over to the care of God *as we understood Him.*

4. Made a searching and fearless moral inventory of ourselves.

5. Admitted to God, to ourselves, and to another human being the exact nature of our wrongs.

6. Were entirely ready to have God remove all these defects of character.

7. Humbly asked Him to remove our shortcomings.

8. Made a list of all persons we had harmed, and became willing to make amends to them all.

9. Made direct amends to such people wherever possible, except when to do so would injure them or others.

10. Continued to take personal inventory and when we were wrong promptly admitted it.

11. Sought through prayer and meditation to improve our conscious contact with God, *as we understood Him,* praying only for knowledge of His will for us and the power to carry that out.

12. Having had a spiritual awakening as the result of these Steps, we tried to carry this message to alcoholics, and to practice these principles in all our affairs.

The Twelve Steps are reprinted with permission of Alcoholics Anonymous World Services, Inc. ("AAWS") Permission to reprint the Twelve Steps does not mean that AAWS has reviewed or approved the contents of this publication, or that AAWS necessarily agrees with the views expressed herein. A.A. is a program of recovery from alcoholism only - use of the Twelve Steps in connection with programs and activities which are patterned after A.A., but which address other problems, or in any other non-A.A. context, does not imply otherwise.

Contact Information for Twelve-Step Programs

Al-Anon/Al-Ateen
http://www.al-anon.alateen.org

Al-Anon Family Group Headquarters, Inc.
1600 Corporate Landing Parkway
Virginia Beach, VA 23454-5617
Telephone: (757) 563-1600
Fax: (757) 563-1655
email: wso@al-anon.org

Al-Anon Family Group Headquarters (Canada), Inc.
275 Slater Street, Suite 900
Ottawa ON K1P 5H9
Telephone: (613) 723-8484
email: afgwso@al-anon.org

Alcoholics Anonymous
http://www.aa.org
A.A. World Services, Inc
P.O. Box 459
Grand Central Station
New York, NY 10163
Telephone: (212) 870-3400

Adult Children of Alcoholic or Dysfunctional Families
www.adultchildren.org
ACA WSO
P.O. Box 3216
Torrance, CA 90510

Telephone: (562) 595-7831

Co-Dependents Anonymous, Inc. (CoDA)
http://www.coda.org
CoDA Fellowship Services Office
P.O. Box 33577
Phoenix, AZ 85067-3577
email: outreach@coda.org

Narconon
http://www.narconon.org/
Narconon is a program dedicated to helping people dependent on drugs or alcohol.

Addictions Victorious
http://www.addvicinc.org/
Celebrate Recovery
http://www.celebraterecovery.com
Christians in Recovery
http://christians-in-recovery.org

About the Author

Diane Jellen was born in Pennsylvania, and after ringing in the 21st century she moved to Florida. The positive energy of the Sunshine State motived Jellen to write her memoir, *My Resurrected Heart: A Codependent's Journey to Healing,* which won the 2015 *Christian Small Publisher Devotional Book of the Year* award.

You can reach Diane at dianejellen@aol.com and read her inspiring blogs at www.dianejellen.com

www.ingramcontent.com/pod-product-compliance
Lightning Source LLC
Chambersburg PA
CBHW021152020426
42331CB00003B/20